MERLION ARTS LIBRARY

LOOKING

—AT—

ART

Copyright © 1991 Merlion Publishing Ltd
First published 1992 by
Merlion Publishing Ltd
2 Bellinger Close
Greenways Business Park
Chippenham
Wiltshire SN15 1BN
UK

2nd printing 1992

Design: Paul Fielder
Series Editor: Charlotte Ryrie

Manufactured in Great Britain by
BPCC Hazells Ltd

ISBN 1 85737 060 0

Cover artwork by Richard Berridge, Paul Fielder and Gwen
Tourret; photography by Mike Stannard.

Artwork on pages 13, 21 by Tim Beer; pages 8, 15, 19, 24, 27, 28–29,
30–31, 33, 38, 41, 43, 53, 57, 64, 66–67, 72, 77, 82, 85, 92, 98–99, 101,
106–107, 108, 116, 117, 119, 147, 149, 151, 152–153, 155, 159, 161, 162–
163, 166–167, 169 by Paul Fielder; pages 10, 17, 97, 102, 114 by Mike
Lacey; pages 51, 59, 81, 84, 91, 96, 111, 122, 129, 131, 133, 137, 145, 177
by Andrew Midgeley; page 23 by Jeremy Plumb; pages 61, 68–69,
74–75, 95, 115, 120–121, 125, 135, 141, 143, 157 by Edward Russell;
pages 6–7, 46–47, 86–87, 126–127 by Gwen and Shirley Tourret and
page 45 by Helen Williams.

Photographs on pages 8, 15, 19, 23, 24, 27, 28–29, 32–33, 38, 41, 43,
49, 53, 54–55, 57, 64, 66–67, 70–71, 72, 77, 82, 85, 92, 98–99, 101,
106–107, 108, 112–113, 116–117, 119, 147, 149, 151, 152–153, 155, 158,
159, 161, 166–167, 168–169, 170–171, 172–173, 174 by Mike Stannard.

MERLION ARTS LIBRARY

LOOKING

AT

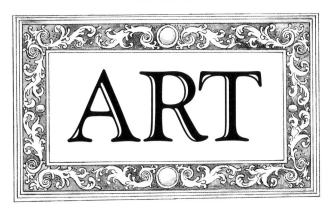

Written by Anthea Peppin

and Helen Williams

Merlion Publishing

CONTENTS

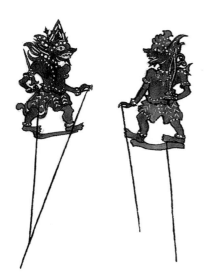

CHAPTER ONE

People in Art

From the earliest times, people have
painted pictures and made figures
from clay and wood. This book shows
you many works of art. They were
created by all kinds of artists, for all sorts
of reasons. Some of the pictures
and sculptures are very old. Others
were made recently.

In this chapter, you can look at pictures
of people. They come from all over the
world. Some are paintings, some are
drawings, some are sculptures. There
are even masks and puppets.

Some of the pictures may make you feel
happy, others may make you feel sad.
Some may make you curious, and some
may make you smile. Look carefully and
see how you feel about each picture.
You don't have to like them all!

There are lots of simple projects for you
to try. Follow the instructions carefully
and look at the photographs and
drawings. You will have fun finding
out that you, too, can be an artist!

All kinds of lines

A quick way to make a picture is with lines. When you look at something like a chair or a table, you imagine there is a line around it. The line isn't really there — your eyes invent it, to separate the object you are looking at from its background. When you want to make a drawing, it is this imaginary line that you put on to your paper. The line shows the shape of the object you are looking at. It is called an outline.

Learning about lines

You can make many different kinds of line — thin, thick, light, dark, smooth, straight, curved. Use a pencil, a wax crayon and a felt-tip pen to draw lines on a sheet of paper. Look at the differences in the lines.

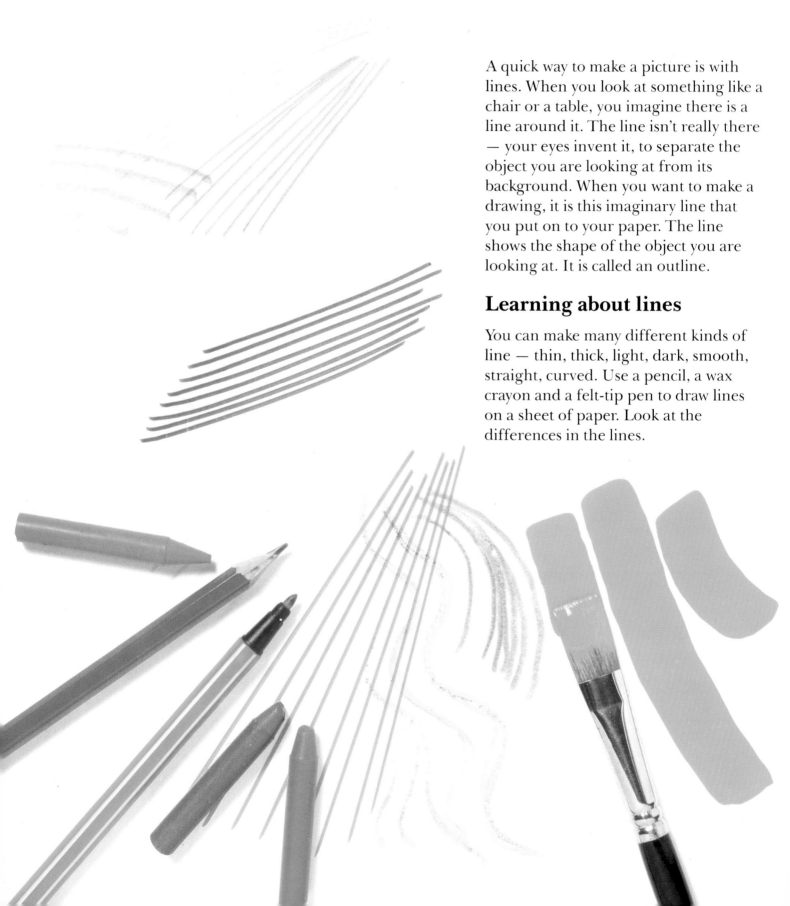

This cave painting of hunters or warriors was found at Valltorta in Spain.

Thick and thin lines

Long ago, cave people covered the walls of their caves with pictures of people and animals. They painted them with large, thick lines. These were probably made with sharpened sticks dipped in coloured earth. The people they painted look strong and bold.

This picture is by the Italian artist, Raphael. It was drawn nearly 500 years ago. He has drawn a young man with black chalk, using many different kinds of line. There is a strong outline around the face and hat. But the hair has been drawn with thin strokes to show it is fine and soft.

Make a drawing of the palm of your hand. Begin with the outline. Then take a pencil with a fine point and fill in as many lines as you can.

'Portrait of a young man' was drawn by the Italian artist, Raphael.

Now try drawing someone's hair, or the folds in their clothes. Keep your collection of line drawings together. You may want to look back at them as you read the next part of the book.

A Portrait of yourself

A portrait is a picture of a person. Artists often paint their own portraits as well as those of other people. A portrait of yourself is called a self-portrait.

Try drawing your self-portrait. You will need a mirror, some paper and a pencil. Sit at a table and prop up the mirror so that you can see yourself easily. Now you can begin to draw your face. First, sketch the positions of your eyes, nose and mouth. Look carefully at your head — notice that your eyes are about

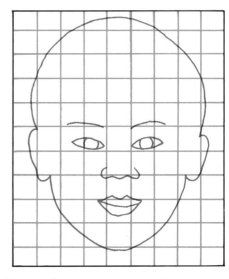

half-way down. How much room does your nose take up? How far is your mouth from your nose?

Shade in the shadows

In real life your face has bumps and hollows. But the picture you are drawing is flat. How do you make your flat picture look more life-like? Look at this self-portrait by the German artist, Albrecht Dürer. He has made his face appear solid by shading in the parts that are in shadow. If you look at your own face in the mirror, you will see that some areas are darker than others. Shade in these areas on your picture, using your pencil. Soon, your picture will stop looking flat and start to look like a real face.

The German artist, Albrecht Dürer, painted this self-portrait when he was only 13.

Portrait of an artist

Rembrandt van Rijn was a famous Dutch artist who lived in the 1600s. He was very popular and painted many portraits of wealthy people. All his life he was his own favourite model, and he painted about 70 self-portraits. The earlier ones show him looking very successful and pleased with life. This one was painted shortly before he died, when he was old and quite poor.

This was the last self-portrait painted by the Dutch artist, Rembrandt van Rijn.

Light and dark

'The Orrery' was painted by the English artist, Joseph Wright.

Many artists look at the effects of light and dark in their paintings. People can look strange and unfamiliar if their faces are in shadow, or if they are lit up by a bright light.

Look at this painting by the English artist, Joseph Wright. It shows some people looking at an orrery. An orrery is

a clockwork model which shows the movements of the planets around the Sun. There is a bright light in the centre of the picture which comes from the model sun. Can you see how it lights up the children's faces? Notice the interesting shadows on the clothes and faces of the other figures.

Paint yourself in shadow

Try painting your face in this dramatic way. You will need a flashlight, a mirror, some paper, paints, brushes, a palette and a pencil. Stand in front of the mirror in a dark room. Shine the flashlight onto your face from above, below and from the side. See how different you look! Then prop up the flashlight so that your hands are free. Begin your picture by sketching in the outlines of your face with a pencil. To paint your face, first mix your skin colour.

Add small amounts of white paint to your skin colour to paint places where your face is lit by the flashlight, and black where it is in shadow. Some shadows contain blue or purple tints as well.

What is form?

You are a solid object. So is a table, a chair or a tree. You are not flat, like a piece of paper. You have form.

We can understand form more easily through touch. Ask some friends to help you with an experiment. First, put some small objects from around your home into a box.

This sculpture by Henry Moore is called 'Recumbent Figure' – a person lying down.

Ask your friends to close their eyes and take turns in picking out an object from the box. How much can they tell you about each form just by turning it around in their hands?

Walk around a sculpture

A sculptor is an artist who enjoys making solid forms, rather than flat paintings. These are called sculptures. This large sculpture was carved from stone by the British sculptor, Henry Moore. You can only see part of the sculpture from looking at this photograph. You really need to walk around it and look at it from several different positions.

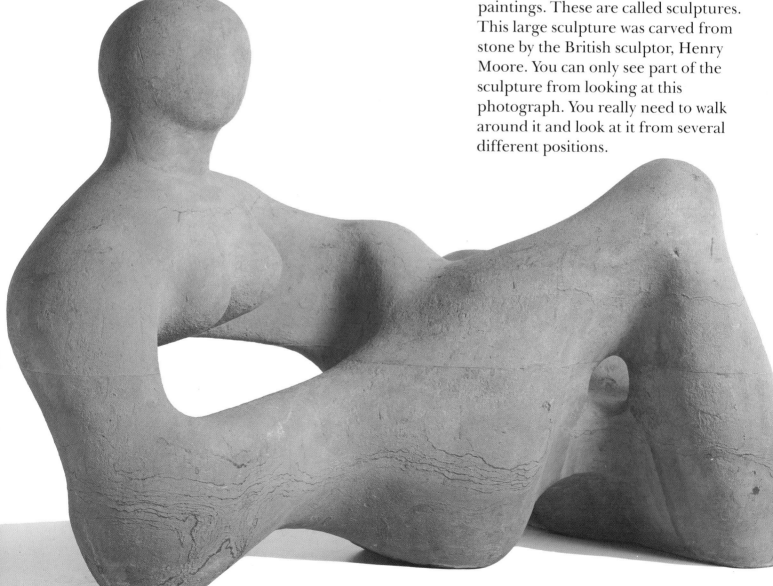

This is a sculpture of an Inuit mother and her child.

All kinds of sculpture

Sculptures can be all shapes and sizes. They can be larger than a house, or small enough to stand on a table. You can make a sculpture from almost anything. An Inuit carved this small sculpture from a soft, heavy stone called soapstone. Can you imagine how it would feel to touch? You can explore sculptures with your fingertips as well as with your eyes.

Make your own sculpture

Most stone is too hard to work on without special tools. If you want to try making a sculpture, begin with a soft material like soap. Find a block of soap, then cover a table with newspaper. Ask which knife you may use and remember to take care — if it's sharp enough to cut the soap, it may also cut you!

Try carving a face or a figure. Keep turning the form around in your hands to see how it changes from all sides. When you are pleased with your sculpture, brush off any scrapings of soap and put it somewhere dry.

Shapes in silhouette

If we draw a simple outline of an object, and then colour it black, we make a silhouette. This shows us the shape of the object.

In Europe during the 1700s, silhouette portraits became popular. The portraits were either painted black or cut out from black paper and put on a white background. They usually showed the profile, or side view, of a person's head. A clever artist could get a good likeness of a person. Sometimes he might even show whole groups of people this way.

The word silhouette comes from the name of a French politician, Étienne de Silhouette, who lived in the 1700s. He was famous for being very mean. His name became used for things which could be made very cheaply. It was much cheaper to have a silhouette portrait made than to have a portrait painted.

This is a silhouette of a man cutting his own silhouette.

These two shadow puppets come from Malaysia.

Shadow stories

We can also make silhouettes with shadows. In some countries, special shadow puppets are used to perform plays. In Malaysia, shadow puppets like these ones are finely carved and decorated. Each puppet has moving joints. Sticks are attached to the back so that the puppets can be operated by hand. A screen is placed in front of the puppets. A light shines behind them to cast a shadow on the screen. The audience sits in front of the screen and watches the silhouettes of the puppets.

A silhouette portrait

Try to make a silhouette portrait of someone you know. First draw their profile. Then you can either paint it black, or cut it out of black paper with scissors. You could use the same technique as the Malaysian puppeteers to help you. Make a screen by hanging up a large piece of white paper or cloth. Place the person you want to copy behind it. Make sure the person is sitting sideways. Then shine a light behind so that a shadow of the person's profile appears on the screen. This makes a silhouette for you to copy.

Asian brushstrokes

'The Hunt' is a book illustration by the Japanese artist, Masayoshi.

A Japanese artist called Masayoshi painted these pictures about 200 years ago. They were painted to illustrate stories in a book. There are lots of people, all busy doing different things. If you look carefully you can also see that each figure is drawn using only two or three separate lines.

Masayoshi used a brush with a fine point. He painted in long strokes without taking his brush off the paper. In some places the lines are thin, but in other places the figures look solid. The thick lines are made by leaning the brush against the paper, and the thin lines are made by drawing with the tip.

This style is good for showing movement, and figures look full of energy. Can you draw in this lively way?

Your own brush drawing

Drawing with a brush can be very difficult. Choose a soft one with a point, or use a special brush pen. First practise making different kinds of strokes. Try making straight and curved lines. Make them thick and thin without taking your brush off the paper. When you feel confident, choose what you are going to draw. See if you can draw a figure using less than six separate strokes.

You can use a pencil instead of a brush, but it must have a broad lead so that you can make thick and thin lines. It is quite difficult to show movement using pencil lines in this way, unless you are already very skilful.

People from Ancient Egypt

'Hunting Fowl in the Marshes' was painted on the wall of the tomb of Nebamun, in Thebes.

Painting things clearly

Why do you think the Ancient Egyptian artists painted people in this strange way? They thought it was important to show images clearly, even if the paintings didn't look absolutely true to life. So they did not paint exactly what they saw, but painted things in the way which seemed most clear to them.

There are other unusual things in this picture. Can you see Nebamun's wife and daughter? The artist has painted them much smaller than Nebamun, to show that he thinks they are less important. There are also many different birds in the picture. How many can you count? Do you think you would see so many different kinds at one time?

An Ancient Egyptian family

Try drawing or painting your own family in this style. You don't have to copy them from real life, but draw them from memory like the Ancient Egyptians did. Use bright colours and include as many details as you can. Who do you think are the most important people in your family? Make them the largest figures in your picture.

Ancient Egyptian artists had an interesting way of painting people. Let's look carefully at this picture. It shows a man called Nebamun, who is hunting birds in the marshes. Notice that we see his head from the side, but his eye is painted as if we are looking at it from the front. Nebamun's legs and feet are shown sideways, too, but his arms and shoulders are turned to face us. Try standing in this position. It's not very comfortable!

What is a caricature?

'King Louis Philippe changing into a pear in 4 stages' was drawn by the French artist, Honoré Daumier.

Have you seen cartoons in newspapers? They often show famous people, such as politicians or movie stars. They are often drawn in an unkind way which exaggerates certain things about them. This type of drawing is called a caricature.

Caricatures are meant to make fun of the people they show. An artist chooses certain features about a person, such as their nose or their teeth, then draws these features in an exaggerated way. If the person is famous for doing something in particular, such as talking too much, the caricature may exaggerate that activity, too.

Here is a well-known French caricature drawn about 150 years ago. It shows a French king turning into a pear. In France at that time it was very rude to call somebody a pear because it meant they were stupid. The artist is making fun of the king, whose name was Louis Philippe, for eating too much. The artist was also suggesting the king was a fool.

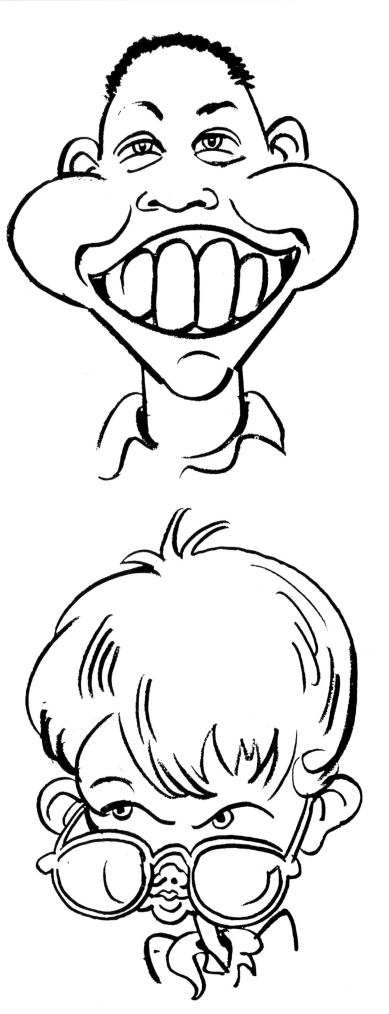

Drawing your own caricature

Try drawing your own caricature. Choose a friend who likes to have fun. Ask yourself what is special about them. Are they tall and skinny? Do their ears stick out? Do they have a funny hairstyle? Do they smile a lot? Perhaps there is something they particularly like doing, such as bicycling, or reading books. When you have decided what to exaggerate, draw your caricature in pencil. The best caricatures are drawn in a very sketchy way without much detail, so try not to put too many lines in your picture. Does the finished picture make you laugh? Does it make your friend laugh, too?

Fantastic faces

Have you ever seen a face made from plants before? An Italian artist called Arcimboldi, who lived in the 1500s, liked to paint faces that were made from plants.

If you look at this painting from far away it just looks like an ordinary picture of a strange man. But when you look more closely, you can see that the man is made from different plants. Can you recognise any of the different fruits, flowers and vegetables? Notice that each plant has been painted with great care. The pear that makes the man's nose looks so real that you almost want to pick it up and eat it!

A plant portrait

Arcimboldi spent a long time painting the plants in his pictures so that they looked life-like. You can create a similar effect by using cut-out photographs from magazines.

You will need a pile of old magazines, a large sheet of paper, some scissors and glue. First, search through the magazines for photographs of fruit, flowers and vegetables. Carefully cut out the ones that you want to use. Decide whether your portrait is going to be a side view or a front view. Then choose some of your photographs and arrange them on the paper in the shape of a face. When you are happy with the result, glue the photographs on to the paper.

'Vertumnus' was painted by the Italian artist, Giuseppe Arcimboldi, for the Hapsburg Emperor, Rudolf.

African masks

The masks on this page come from Africa. They were made by tribesmen to wear on special occasions, or ceremonies. Each ceremony celebrates a particular time of year, or marks a special event, such as a wedding, or a funeral. There is usually dancing and music, and bright costumes are worn. The dances often tell stories about the tribe's history. Different tribes have always had different styles of mask and decoration.

Many African tribes are very talented at wood carving. This mask of a hyena's head is carefully carved. Other masks may be decorated with paint or feathers. Some masks were meant to make people laugh. Others were sad, or frightening. How does this decorated mask make you feel?

This is a ritual mask from the Yoruba tribe.

An Ibo tribesman carved this hyena's head mask.

This decorated mask from the Ivory Coast was made 100 years ago.

Making your own mask

You can easily make your own mask from cardboard. You will also need some paint, and a collection of other materials for decoration. You might like to add feathers, buttons, leaves or scraps of cloth. Use whatever you can find! First decide what shape you want the mask to be and cut it out.

Then make your eye holes. Round eye holes can make your mask look surprised. Eye holes which slant downwards can make it look sad. Holes slanting upwards can seem angry. Try different shapes on a piece of paper before you mark them on the card and cut them out. You can cut out holes for your mouth and your nose, or you can paint them. You can even glue different things on to make a mouth and nose.

It is fun sticking lots of different materials onto your mask to make it interesting. But make sure that all the glue is dry before you start to paint. African masks were often painted in vivid patterns. Your mask can also look powerful if you just use one bold colour.

Let's look at colour

The world is full of colours — they are everywhere we look. Most artists are interested in using colour. They can make almost any colour they wish by mixing together their paints.

The three primary colours

Red, blue and yellow are called primary colours. This means that we can't make them by mixing together any other colours.

But if we mix primary colours together we can make many, many more colours! For example, when we mix red and yellow paint together, we make orange. But we don't always make the same colour orange.

Mixing colours

Put some yellow paint on your palette and add a tiny amount of red paint to the yellow. Mix them together with a little water. With a clean brush, paint a stripe of the colour you have made near the edge of your paper. Now mix a little more red into the paint on your palette. Paint a stripe of this new colour next to the first. Carry on adding red and painting stripes. You'll see that red and yellow can make many different colours — from a golden yellow to an orangey red.

Try the same experiment with yellow and blue paint, to make lots of different greens. Then mix blue and red paint to make several purples.

Count the colours

This painting by the French painter Auguste Renoir contains many beautiful colours. Make a list of every kind of colour you can find in the painting.

'The Children's Afternoon at Wargemont' was painted by the French painter, Auguste Renoir.

Colour mixing

The primary colours — red, blue and yellow — cannot be made by mixing other colours together. The secondary colours — green, orange and purple — are made by mixing two primary colours. Blue and yellow mixed together make green. Red and yellow make orange. Red and blue make purple.

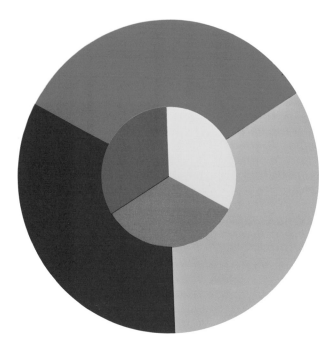

Complementary colours are like opposite colours. They stand out from each other and do not blend together. Red and green are complementary. Yellow and purple are complementary, so are blue and orange. Look at the colour wheel. It will help you to see which colours are primary, secondary and complementary.

Using tiny coloured dots

This painting is by the French painter, Georges Seurat. He tried different ways of mixing colours. Instead of mixing

them before he painted, he used tiny dots of primary colours next to each other. He painted green grass by using blue and yellow dots together.

'Sunday afternoon on the Isle of the Grande Jatte' was painted by the French artist, Georges Seurat.

Sometimes he put in a few dots of complementary colour as well. He put a few dots of red in the grass because he thought it would make the green stand out more. You can see this clearly in the magnified picture.

Try using coloured dots for yourself. Paint some red and blue dots together. How far away do you have to stand for them to look purple? The smaller you make the dots, the nearer you will be able to stand.

Colour your mood!

'A maid combing a woman's hair' painted by the French artist, Edgar Degas.

Colour is powerful! Looking at colours can make you feel happy, sad, calm or excited. In other words, colours can change your mood.

Most artists think of reds and yellows as 'warm' colours. This may be because they are the colours of fire or the Sun — which are both hot! In this painting by Edgar Degas, a woman is leaning back in her chair while another woman brushes her long hair. The artist has used mainly reds and oranges. Perhaps he wanted us to feel that the room is warm and the woman is relaxed.

Changing tones

Painters can change the mood of a painting by making the colours lighter or darker. This is called changing their tone. We use black and white to change the tone of the primary colours.

Put some red paint on your palette. Paint a stripe of red near the edge of your paper. Now add a tiny spot of black paint to your red. Paint a stripe of the new colour next to the old one.

Carry on painting more stripes, adding a little more black each time. As you add black, the colour becomes richer and darker. You might want to use deep colours like these if you are painting a night-time scene.

Bright, sunny yellows

Wash your brush and experiment with yellow paint. This time, add white a little at a time. The strong yellow will become lighter and clearer in tone. These kinds of yellow colours can give a painting a feeling of sunshine.

Dull, sad blues

Now mix up some grey paint. Start with white and add black a little at a time, until you get grey. Then put some blue paint on another part of your palette. Paint a stripe of blue on to your paper. Now add a small amount of grey to the blue. Paint some stripes as you did before, mixing in a little more grey each time.

Adding grey makes colours lose their brightness and become dull. You can use dull tones like these to paint a cold, rainy day. Dull colours give a painting a sad mood.

Paint your mood

Artists have to decide on the mood of a picture before they begin to paint. Then they choose tones to match that feeling. You can make a mood picture of your own. Think of things that make you happy and excited, angry and upset. You don't have to paint a scene. Just use colour to show how you are feeling.

'The Scream' was painted by the Norwegian artist, Edvard Munch.

Colours and feelings

A man stands at the edge of a bridge. His hands are clasped to his head. His eyes are huge and staring and his mouth is opened wide to scream. His face is crooked and twisted. Behind him, the landscape is a swirling mass of bright lines and the clouds are the colour of blood.

The picture is called 'The Scream'. It was painted by the Norwegian artist, Edvard Munch. Everything in the picture expresses chaos. The colours of the scenery are bold and not what we would expect. They seem to be copying the distress of the screaming man. The colours shock us.

Frightening colours

Munch is not simply trying to paint some figures in a landscape. He is using shapes and colours to express a deep feeling. His painting expresses fear. Something terrible has happened, but we do not know what it is. Munch was one of several artists who became known as Expressionists. They felt strongly that paintings could show people worrying and suffering, as well as showing the beautiful things in life.

Powerful colours

The smaller picture was painted by the Spanish artist, Pablo Picasso, in 1937. He has used powerful colours to make us look at the unhappiness of the crying woman. Sometimes when people are very upset, we say that they 'go to pieces'

'Woman Weeping' was painted by the Spanish artist, Pablo Picasso.

or are 'broken up' by their sadness. Picasso's woman looks as if she really is broken into pieces.

Can you see the jagged blue and white shapes of the woman's mouth as she bites onto her handkerchief? Picasso was the first artist to use such an unrealistic style. He was the leader of a group of artists called Cubists. Cubists divided their pictures up into shapes. Then they moved and overlapped the shapes to give an unusual view of their subject.

Individual portraits

When somebody has their portrait painted, they like to be made to look their best. Kings and queens and rulers are usually painted to look very important. They may be wearing their grandest robes and jewels, or dressed in a smart uniform. Perhaps they will be standing in a splendid room, or have part of a grand building in the background. A portrait does not usually show somebody wearing ordinary clothes or looking plain, even if this is how they really look in everyday life.

An uncomfortable dress

Here is a picture of Mariana, the wife of Philip IV, a king of Spain in the 1600s. The Spanish artist, Velasquez, has painted the queen dressed in a magnificently decorated costume. Even her hair is richly decorated. Do you think Mariana is happy to be wearing this dress for her portrait? If you look carefully at her face, you might guess that she is bored and uncomfortable!

'Portrait of Mariana of Austria, Queen of Spain' was painted by the Spanish artist, Diego Rodriguez de Silva y Velasquez.

'Girl in a red dress' was painted by the American artist, Ammi Phillips.

Portraits of ordinary people

Ordinary people can be made to look beautiful, or important, as well. Look at this picture of an ordinary Japanese girl. The artist has shown her wearing flowing clothes which fall gracefully around her. The colours are very delicate. The flower behind the girl is also very graceful and delicate. The combination of shapes and colours make us think the girl is very beautiful.

The little American girl in the picture looks pretty in her best clothes. She has her favourite animal with her. She looks serious. Perhaps she is trying very hard to keep still!

Your own portrait

If you wanted to have your portrait painted, how would you like to look? Would you like to look very grand, or very beautiful? Perhaps you would like to look very clever, or very rich. Think about what clothes you would wear, and what other details you would like to see included.

'Woman and chrysanthemums' is a colour woodcut by the Japanese artist, Utagawa Kuniyoshi.

Miniature pictures

This tiny portrait, 'Girl with apple', was painted by the English artist, Isaac Oliver.

Do you have a picture of someone who is special to you? If you do, it's probably a photograph. Long ago, before cameras were invented, people sometimes treasured tiny paintings. Some of them were so small that they could fit into the palm of your hand. Sometimes, people attached them to gold chains to hang round their necks.

English miniature portraits

These tiny English portraits were painted about 400 years ago. They were painted on vellum, which is fine calf's skin. The paintings are the same size as they are shown here. The little girl is dressed in her best clothes. The picture has been enlarged to show you the beautifully painted lace on her collar, and the pattern on her dress. The artist must have used a brush with only one or two hairs to paint such fine detail.

A handsome young man

Perhaps this picture of a smart young Englishman was a present for his lover. He looks very romantic leaning against the rose tree. You can tell from his fine clothes that he was rich. These paintings usually show people from wealthy families. It was expensive to have a miniature portrait painted.

Persian miniatures

There is a picture of a Persian miniature painting on page 44 in this book. These pictures were made for wealthy rulers who kept them in a book, like an album. Persian artists used brushes made from fine hairs from kittens or squirrels when they painted these tiny pictures. They painted the colours in different layers, and even used gold to paint fine details on the top layer. It could take an artist sixty days to complete just one small painting.

Make your own miniature

Try drawing a miniature portrait of your favourite person. Mark a circle or oval on a piece of white card. It should not be more than five centimetres across. Use very sharp coloured pencils and work slowly and carefully. You will not get good results if you rush.

Miniature silhouettes were also popular in Europe a hundred years ago. You can find out how to make a silhouette on page 16.

'Portrait of a Young Man' was painted by the English artist, Nicholas Hilliard.

Giant figures

The Statue of Liberty stands outside New York, USA.

Works of art can be enormous. When we think of art, we often think of pictures hung on walls, or objects in special galleries. In fact, many works of art can be seen in more everyday places.

The Statue of Liberty

The Statue of Liberty is a huge figure of a woman carrying a flaming torch. This figure stands in the harbour of New York, in the USA. It suggests that travellers are entering a country where freedom is important. The statue was actually made by a Frenchman just over 100 years ago. It was made from 300 different pieces which were sent by boat from France to New York. It must have been a difficult job to piece them all together!

A huge statue of Buddha

This giant Japanese figure of Buddha is 13 metres high. Buddha was a prince who gave up all his riches. He then taught people a better way of life. These teachings became the foundations of Buddhism, one of the world's great religions.

Look around your local town. What different kinds of art can you see? Are they large or small? Think about how the images were made, and why they are there. What would you like to see?

The Great Buddha is at Kamokora, in Japan.

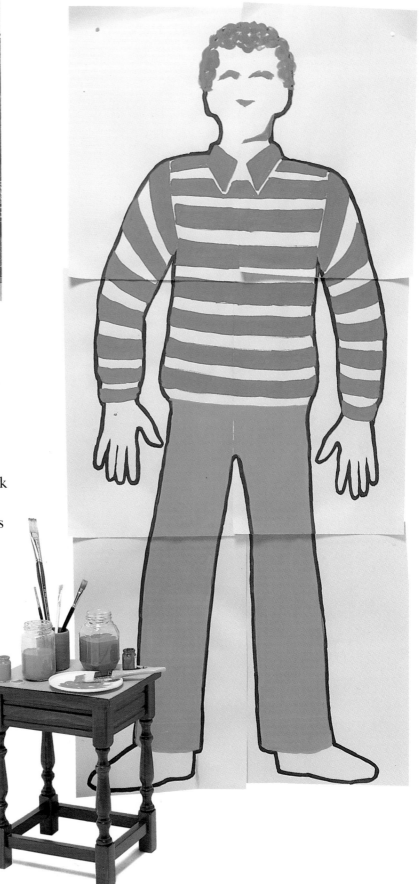

Make a life-size figure

You can make a large figure, too. You need a big piece of paper. You might be able to find an old roll of wallpaper, or join several small sheets of paper together. Ask a friend or a member of your family to lie down on the paper, and draw round them. Use a thick, black pen. You will then have an outline to colour in. Try and get the face to look as realistic as possible. You can paint the clothes with bright colours and interesting patterns. When you have finished the figure, cut it out. Does it look like a real person when you pin it on a wall?

Crowds of people

‘Children's Games’ was painted by the Flemish artist, Pieter Brueghel the Elder.

There are many ways of painting crowds of people. Some artists paint each person in a crowd clearly. Other artists only show the details of the people in the front of the picture. This picture of crowds of children playing games is full of detail. The people in the distance look just as real as the ones in the front of the picture. The artist, Pieter Brueghel, painted in Flanders in the 1500s. You can learn a lot about life in a Flemish town at that time from looking at this picture. You can see the clothes people wore, and the games they played. Do you recognise any of the games? Do you play any similar games?

Faces in the front row

Look at the other picture of a crowd. The Italian artist, Duccio, has painted it so you only see the faces of the front row. You know that there are other people behind them because you can see the tops of their heads. When Duccio was painting in Italy, in the 1400s, most pictures were painted to illustrate stories about the Christian religion. Artists wanted to show the main characters in each story, but did not always think it was important to paint all the other people in such detail.

Make your own crowd picture

First you must plan your picture of a crowd. What sort of crowd do you want to show? How many people will there be? Will people be spaced out or packed closely together? You could choose people at a sporting event, at school, or in a busy street. What sort of clothes will they be wearing?

Then you need to decide on your viewing point. If you are looking straight at a crowd you may only see the front row in detail. If you are looking down at a crowd, as if you are on a stage and they are the audience, you will be able to see what the people farthest away are doing. Draw the front row first. Do not forget that people in the distance will appear smaller than people in the front of your picture.

'Jesus opens the eyes of a man born blind' was painted by the Italian artist, Duccio di Buoninsegna.

Images from Islam

'Barbad playing music to Khusraw' is one of a series of 14 miniature paintings by the Persian artist, Mir Sayyid Ali.

Islam is the religion of the Muslim people. Muslims pray in a mosque where the walls are often richly decorated. These decorations include brightly coloured patterns, pictures of flowers and flowing Arabic writing. The floors of mosques are covered with carpets and rugs of bright colours and complicated designs.

There are no pictures showing people in mosques. But there are many beautiful and life-like paintings of people in other kinds of Islamic art. In the 1500s, Muslim rulers employed artists to paint detailed pictures showing life in the royal courts and palaces. Pictures that told stories were also popular.

A busy scene

In this painting from Persia, you can see people doing many different things. Musicians are playing love songs to a prince. A man with a hawk stands beside an archer. Other characters are carrying cloth, or offering food and drink. Can you see a baby? Can you tell what everybody is doing? You can also see many different patterns which are typical of Islamic art. Can you see an example of Arabic writing?

The artist, Mir Sayyid Ali, has painted the decorative patterns very carefully. He has also taken a lot of trouble to paint people's clothes in great detail. But all the faces have exactly the same expression. Can you think of a reason for this?

Make your own Islamic pattern

Pattern making is more difficult than it looks! To start with, try copying a pattern from the border of this page. You could trace the pattern, or copy it onto squared paper.

When you have made the outlines you can colour them in. Look carefully at the colours that have been used on this page and in the main picture. Try to match these colours by mixing your own paints. Every time that a shape is repeated in your pattern you must use the same colour.

If you feel confident, you can design your own Islamic pattern. Think carefully about what colours to include, and what shapes to use. Islamic artists often combined shapes from plants and flowers with squares, diamonds, rectangles and stars.

CHAPTER TWO

Nature in Art

Artists have always been inspired by the natural world around them. Some artists try to show the beauty of animals and plants by copying their appearance as closely as possible. Many others are more interested in showing how they feel about nature.

Nature can be frightening and powerful as well as calm and beautiful. Some of the pictures here express great turmoil and energy. Others describe nature's glorious colours and shapes.

Pictures of animals and plants have been used all over the world for decoration. In this chapter, you can look at printed and carved animals, as well as paintings and drawings. You will also learn where colour really comes from. Discover different styles of painting and drawing and then try them out for yourself!

Fruit and flowers

'Still life with fruit and flowers' was painted by the Dutch artist, Jan van Huysum.

Some pictures of fruits and flowers look so real that you want to touch and smell them. To get this realistic effect, artists spend a long time arranging and looking at the objects they are going to paint. The finished picture is called a still life.

The grapes in this still life look ripe and good to eat. The Dutch artist, Jan van Huysum, has captured their texture and their colour so well that the grapes look real. You can see the gloss on their skins, and you can even make out their pips where the light is shining through them. Can you see any insects?

A whole year to paint one picture

The date on this painting is 1736–37. This means that the painting took over a year to finish. The artist has been very careful to add every little detail. Because he took so long, his picture shows a mixture of flowers which don't all open at the same time of year.

A pleasing design

The Japanese flower picture was also painted in the 1700s. But it is completely different. The artist, Kitagawa Utamaro, is not trying to make the flowers and insect look real. He is more interested in making a pleasing design on the page. You can count the number of colours that he has used. The picture looks flat and there is no feeling that the flowers are real.

Paint a still life picture

You will need paints and a very fine brush. At first, choose something simple to paint. Try painting one or two pieces of fruit and a few flowers.

'Balloon-flower with other plants and cicada' was painted by the Japanese artist, Kitagawa Utamaro.

Spend some time looking carefully at the objects you have chosen. Are they the same colour all over? Are they shiny or dull? Is any part of your arrangement in shadow? Mix your colours before you start to paint.

Wind and water

Think of the different kinds of movement you can see in a windy landscape or a stormy sea. Artists have tried many ways of capturing this movement on paper.

Moving water

'The hollow of the deep sea wave' was painted by the Japanese artist, Hokusai.

The big wave in this picture by the Japanese artist, Hokusai, looks forceful and full of energy. As the wave rises, a mass of foam is thrown violently from the main body of water. The flying foam looks like fluttering birds being hurled from the wave into the sky.

Hokusai has used different types of line to show the different movements in the wave. He used strong, bold lines to show the force of the wave. He used short, broken lines to show the movement of the foam on the water. In the background is the great mountain, Mount Fuji, but the dramatic movement of the sea makes the mountain look tiny and seem unimportant.

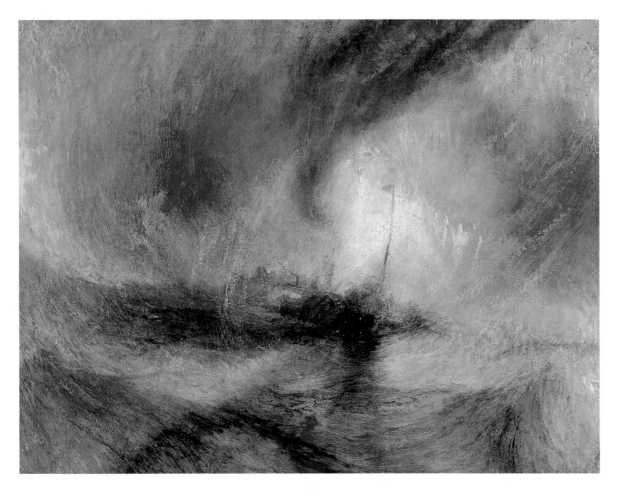

Snowstorm: Steamboat off a Harbour's Mouth was painted by the English artist JMW Turner.

Stormy weather

In the picture on this page, you can almost feel the waves crashing and hear the wind screaming. The English artist, Turner, painted the picture after watching the sea in bad weather. He had to be tied to the mast of a ship so that he wasn't washed overboard! He was fascinated by the movement he saw in the wind and the water.

Drawing movement in nature

Try and capture movement on paper for yourself by drawing a tree being blown by the wind. First, study a tree in the wind. What sort of movement does it make? Is it being blown by a gentle breeze or a strong gale?

Some movements seem like slow and graceful actions. Others may be violent. You may even see awkward and clumsy movements. Think carefully about the kind of lines you need to make when you are painting different actions.

The Power of nature

'The Wreck of The Hope' was painted by the German artist, Caspar-David Friedrich.

When a natural disaster happens today, we often see a film or photograph of it in the news. When the pictures shown here were painted, the artists had to paint a disaster from other people's descriptions.

This picture of a ship caught in icebergs shows us a real event which the German artist, Caspar-David Friedrich, painted

from his imagination. A ship was sailing in the Arctic Ocean when it became trapped in the ice. The ice froze harder and harder.

As the ice froze, it slowly crushed the ship to pieces. If you look carefully, you can see small pieces of the ship sticking out between great slabs of ice. Do you think the picture is frightening?

Storm collage

You can create an exciting stormy picture with cut-out paper. Try and find as many papers with different textures as you can. The idea is to stick down paper shapes to make a special kind of picture, called a collage.

First, make a simple sketch of a storm on a large sheet of paper. Use bold shapes and don't include too much detail. Now, decide what colours you want for each part of your picture and then cut out the shapes. Arrange all the pieces carefully onto your sketch. Then glue them down. You can add more pieces on top until you are happy with your stormy collage.

Colour from nature

People have always wanted to use the colours they see around them in their lives. The earliest people decorated their bodies, their dishes and their weapons, as well as using different colours in their wall paintings. Now, we can walk into a shop and buy trays of brilliantly coloured paints which are probably made in a laboratory. But for thousands of years, all colours came from animals, vegetables or minerals. We call these natural colour's pigments.

Some colours can be made from earths which have been tinted with natural materials, such as iron. To make these special earths into paint, they are ground to a fine powder and mixed with something sticky, like egg yolk or oil.

Precious stones

Some of the brightest colours have always come from stones. It is rare to find much blue paint in early paintings, because the brightest blue, ultramarine, was very expensive. Ultramarine comes from a semi-precious stone called lapis lazuli. The best lapis lazuli has always been found in a mine in northern Afghanistan.

Vermilion is a red pigment and one of the longest lasting colours. It comes from a rare mineral called cinnabar, which is crushed and ground to a fine powder. Cinnabar was once so precious that the Ancient Romans used to transport it from mines in Spain under armed guard.

Colours from animals

Some colours were made from the crushed bodies of animals. Red pigment came from the dried bodies of female cochineal beetles. These beetles were only found in Mexico and South America. This red pigment only became available in other countries after the 1500s, when Europeans brought it from South America. The Ancient Romans even made purple from shells.

Colours from plants

Some of the commonest paint colours have always come from plants. A deep blue can be made from the crushed leaves of the woad plant that grows all over southern Europe and Asia. A bright golden yellow, called saffron yellow, comes from crocus flowers. Crushed berries and seeds can also provide bright colours. You can even make yellow from onion skins. Plant dyes like these tend to fade in sunlight, so they are not often used today.

Poisonous colours

Some colours are poisonous if they are eaten. For thousands of years, painters made a bright yellow called orpiment from the poison arsenic. It is too dangerous to use any more. A clear white paint can be made from poisonous lead powder. Lead paint is now supplied as a thick paste so that you can't breathe in any particles.

Warm and cold colours

'The Allotments' was painted by the Dutch artist, Vincent van Gogh.

What colours do you think of when you think of nature? Do you think of green leaves and grass, or brown earth and branches? Or do you think of blue sky and sea, or yellow sun and sand? It will probably depend on where you live. Can you tell where the pictures on these two pages come from by looking at the colours?

Cool blues and greens

The Dutch artist, Vincent van Gogh, painted the picture above in France. He mainly used pale blues, greens and yellows. The painting gives the impression of a cool summer's day in northern France.

Colour and movement

Van Gogh was fascinated with the colours he saw in nature. By painting different colours with short, thick brushstrokes, he believed he could capture the mood of the landscape he was painting. Do you think he succeeded in this painting?

If you look at the sky, you can see how van Gogh used his brush. There are lots of slightly different shades of blue and yellow, painted with swirling brushstrokes. The cool colours make the sky seem restless, as if rain were about to fall.

Warm golden colours

Do you get a different feeling from this painting? It was painted by an Indian artist, called Abul Hasan, who has also chosen colours which blend well together. But whereas van Gogh used a cold, blue-green, this artist painted with a warm, golden green. Although nearly all the animals and birds are moving busily, the soft colours make the picture seem warm and peaceful.

Shades of green

Try making warm and cold shades of green. Take some blue paint and some yellow paint, and mix them in a small pot to make green. Paint several broad stripes in the centre of a sheet of paper.

Put half of your green into a second pot and mix a little yellow paint into it. Paint a stripe of this new colour on the left side of your green stripes. Now mix a little blue into the other pot. Paint a broad stroke of this colour on the right side of your original green stripes. Keep adding a little more blue to your

'Squirrels in a Chennar Tree' was painted by the Indian artist, Abul Hasan.

blue-green pot, and a little more yellow to the other pot. Every time you change the colour, paint a fresh stripe.

Colours from life

Many birds have brightly coloured feathers. Some animals have skins with striking patterns. But most animals are simply coloured so that they don't stand out from their surroundings.

A life-like hare

Some artists can make even the dullest colours look interesting. The German artist, Albrecht Dürer, produced many fine drawings and paintings. He believed that it was important to observe and study animals and nature closely. He often made dozens of sketches of the same creature. This hare is so life-like that you almost want to pick it up from the paper and stroke it.

'The Hare' was painted by the German artist, Albrecht Dürer.

Types of paint

Dürer obviously studied the hare extremely carefully before he painted it. How many different shades of brown can you see in the fur? Dürer has coloured the hare with two different types of paint. He has used watercolour in some places, and gouache in others. Watercolour is a light, see-through type of paint. Gouache is a much thicker paint. Gouache helped Dürer to get a heavier effect than the watercolour, even though he used exactly the same shade of brown.

Realistic colours

The American artist, John James Audubon, painted over 400 pictures of North American birds. Audubon has exactly matched the white of this heron's feathers, and the yellow and brown of its legs. Do you find it as appealing as Dürer's hare? Audubon's birds were painted for a book. He wanted to show the accurate colours and details of every bird in North America. He was not interested in making pleasing pictures to hang on a wall.

'A Great White Heron' was painted by the American artist, John James Audubon.

Nature's brighter colours

You can paint a colourful picture from nature to treasure! You will need a watercolour paintbox and a notepad. Go out and look for butterflies on a bright day. They will not stay still long enough for you to paint them, so just make some sketches at first.

Sketch the shape of the butterfly, and mark the patterns on its wings. Put blobs of paint on your sketches to show you what colours to use when you start

painting. If your colours don't look very life-like make some notes, too. Later on, use your sketches and notes to guide you. Carefully paint your butterfly.

Animal patterns

This design comes from an ancient British manuscript.

The first books ever made were written by hand. They had beautiful illustrations on nearly every page. Pictures were important because few people could read. The earliest British books, which we call illuminated manuscripts, were made by monks about 1,300 years ago.

The pictures on these two pages come from an early British book called the Lindisfarne Gospels. Strange animal shapes weave in and out of each other. They form a pattern of complicated knots and links. If you look closely, you can trace a single strand of the pattern as it winds its way in and out of all the other strands. This type of page is often called a carpet page.

Copy an animal pattern

Try and copy one of these interweaving animal patterns. Take a sheet of white paper and some brightly coloured felt pens. You don't have to use the colours we have shown. Concentrate on copying just one of the animals at first.

When you feel confident, try and make up your own patterns. You can use as many strands of colours as you like. See how complicated your patterns can be! You could join up your patterns to make a colourful border like the one on this page.

Nature from the imagination

A tiger crashes through the jungle. His eyes are opened wide, his teeth are bared in a snarl. His stripy tail is curling and lashing against the undergrowth. Lightning is flashing in the distance, and the rain is pouring down.

This sounds like a very frightening scene. But in this painting by the French artist, Henri Rousseau, there is no feeling of danger. Everything seems still, like a moment from a dream. Rousseau is not trying to show us something that is really happening. He had never visited a jungle and he might not even have seen a tiger. He is more interested in looking at colours, shapes and patterns.

Look how the dark green leaves at the bottom of the picture overlap the thin stripes of grass. As your eyes move to the left, the grass shapes become wider and stronger. The pattern that they make partly covers the tiger's stripes.

Painting patterns

Rousseau has painted the grass and leaves in layers, one on top of another. This suggests that the tiger is in the middle of the jungle, behind the leaves. But look at the way the back half of its body is on top of the grass, while the front half is behind. There is no feeling of distance. Everything looks flat. Do you think the tiger looks like a cardboard cut-out?

Create a tropical forest

Henri Rousseau worked as a customs officer. Painting pictures was his hobby. Many of his pictures show animals from far-away places. Try painting a picture of a tropical forest for yourself, even if you have never seen one.

Think about the shapes and patterns of leaves and make up some exotic plants. They don't have to be realistic! Mix lots of different greens, yellows and browns, and then paint different shapes. Your plants could bend and curve as though they are moving in the breeze. Why not add one or two cut-out animals?

'Tropical Storm with a Tiger' was painted by the French artist, Henri Rousseau.

Let's look at shape

When we draw, we often start with the outside line of a shape. This is called the outline. You can see the shape of an object more clearly if you cut it out of paper. Try cutting a snail shape from thick paper, without drawing the animal first. In other words, use your scissors instead of a pencil. You don't need to cut the whole shape at once. You could make the shell first, then add the head, neck and body later. Check that all the pieces fit together, then stick them on to a large sheet of card.

You might like to make a shape collage of a group of animals. Give them an environment to live in, like a forest or a desert.

This collage by the French artist, Henri Matisse, is called 'The Snail'.

Making a snail out of shapes

The collage above was made by a French artist called Henri Matisse. He began by painting large sheets of paper with bright colours. Then he cut or tore them into shapes. Matisse arranged the shapes very carefully on his background. At first he only pinned them down. When he was happy with the arrangement of shapes and colours he stuck the pieces down.

Matisse called his collage 'The Snail'. Look carefully and you will see why. Let your eyes follow the colours, starting with the green in the top corner on the right. The shapes inside the orange border trace a spiral — just like the shape of a snail's shell. Is your animal collage anything like this one by Matisse?

Shapes and patterns

'View of Salisbury Cathedral from the Bishop's Grounds' was painted by the English artist, John Constable.

When artists are painting trees and plants, they often concentrate on the shape and pattern of leaves. Some pictures of trees are painted in a realistic way. Other pictures of nature don't look at all real at first.

Realistic leaves

Look at this painting by the English artist, John Constable. His trees look solid and real. The painting is almost like a beautifully arranged colour photograph. Yet if you look closely, you can see that every leaf is exactly alike.

It would take an artist far too long to paint the trees exactly as they are in nature, where every leaf is different. Instead, they copy the shape and pattern of the leaves.

Recognizing shapes

The Swiss artist, Paul Klee, paints in a completely different way! His trees do not look at all real, but they are easy to recognize. He has painted trees as simple shapes. Some of the shapes curve and bend like graceful young trees. Others are hard and clipped, like tall trees in a city park. Paintings like this look simple at first. In fact, Klee has studied the landscape just as carefully as Constable. Both painters had a great understanding of the patterns found in nature which they expressed in different ways.

Look at leaf patterns

Make a collection of leaves from plants around you. They will all be different shapes. Some will be long and thin. Some will have jagged edges. Some will be rounded. Look at the patterns on the leaves, too. Are they made of a few strong lines or many fine lines?

Printing patterns

Choose leaves which have clear patterns and shapes. Paint over the rough side of the leaf with thick paint. Then press it down onto the paper.

'Park near L' was painted by the Swiss artist, Paul Klee.

Mosaics

Mosaics are pictures or patterns made from small pieces of coloured stone, marble or glass. Mosaics last for a long time because these materials wear away very slowly. They have been used as wall or floor decorations in different parts of the world for thousands of years.

Roman mosaics

Some beautiful mosaics have been discovered at Pompeii, in Italy. Pompeii was a Roman town that was buried in ash when a volcano called Mount Vesuvius erupted about 2,000 years ago. The Pompeiian mosaic in the picture

This Roman mosaic was discovered at Pompeii, in Italy.

shows marine life which can still be caught in the warm waters of the Mediterranean Sea. Each tiny coloured square was chipped by hand from slabs of marble or stone. The squares were laid one at a time onto a layer of cement.

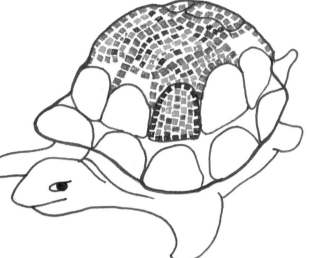

Make a paper mosaic

You will need sheets of different coloured paper or card, scissors and glue. Use one of the sheets of paper as the backing for your mosaic. Decide what animal or plant shape you are going to make. Then sketch its outline on your backing sheet. Cut out lots of squares from your coloured papers. Starting in the middle of your picture and working outwards, stick each square onto the backing paper. Leave a small gap between each square.

A jigsaw mosaic

Some mosaics were made from large pieces of marble cut into different shapes. These pieces were then fitted together like a jigsaw puzzle. Why not try this method, too? Draw a simple shape of an animal, like this macaw. Mark different sections on its body. Put your drawing on top of five different coloured sheets of paper.

Cut round each section of your drawing, making sure that you cut through every layer of paper. Then separate all the pieces, and fit them together using a different colour for each section. You will be able to make five mosaics.

Natural textures

The surface of every object has its own special look and feel. This is called its texture. A log of wood has a rough texture. But the surface of a pebble is smooth. Texture is a very important part of many artists' work.

Textures to touch

Find out more about texture by making a collection of objects with different surfaces. Look for objects made from wood, cloth, metal and stone. Try to find objects that are hard, soft, smooth and rough. Put your collection on a table. Now close your eyes and handle each object in turn. Can you recognize the textures of the objects by feeling them?

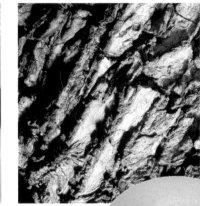

Looking at texture

We don't always have to touch something to understand its texture. Sometimes we only need to look. The photographs above show four familiar surfaces. We can tell which is cold and hard, and which is rough and knobbly, just by looking at them. Our eyes and our memory tell us what to expect.

Magnifying texture

We can use photographs to explore texture in detail. A camera can be used like a magnifying glass. It can show us the tiny details on the surface of a butterfly's wing or a bird's feather. Try looking at your collection of objects through a magnifying glass. What new textures can you discover?

Painting texture

Photographers can take close-up pictures of a surface and show us its texture. But some artists can create textures with paint. They can paint rough wood or soft fur which looks real enough to touch! Here are some ideas for exploring texture yourself.

Mix some thick paints together. Put the mixture on to your paper with quick strokes using a large, dry brush. Try to make a rough, scratchy texture.

Add more water to the paint. Make your paper damp with a wet sponge. Load your brush with paints and drip blobs on to the damp paper. Watch the paint spread out into velvety patches.

Rub a candle or a wax crayon across a sheet of paper. Now brush paint over the whole sheet. The waxy areas will show through the paint. Find out how many other textures you can make, using paint and crayon.

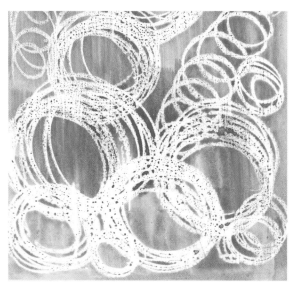

Painting fur

The dog in the picture above was painted by the Flemish artist, Jan van Eyck. See how much care he has taken in painting the texture of the dog's fur. Can you imagine how it would feel to touch? The fur at the bottom of the woman's dress looks even softer.

You might like to try making a very careful painting of a texture like fur or feathers. You could use a magnifying glass to help you see the details — and a small, fine brush to help you paint them.

'The Arnolfini Marriage' was painted by the Flemish artist, Jan van Eyck.

Designs from nature

This tile was designed by the English artist, William de Morgan.

The artists of the pictures on this page have not tried to make them life-like. They have made patterns to fit particular shapes, and they have used plant and animal forms as the pieces of their patterns.

Animal tiles

The English lizard tile on this page was designed about 100 years ago by an English artist called William de Morgan. You can see how the shape of the animals has been made to fit into the square shape of the tile. Tiles often have the same design in each corner so that they fit together to make a continuous pattern.

Repeating patterns

This picture shows a design for fabric. The design was also created about 100 years ago, by an Englishman called William Morris. He liked to design complicated patterns out of natural curves and shapes.

Look at the way the shapes are carefully placed so that the pattern repeats itself. Do you think the plants and birds look real? Can you find any straight lines in the design? William Morris never used any completely straight lines because he could find none in nature.

This fabric design by William Morris is called 'Strawberry Thief'.

Design a pattern to fit a square

You need a piece of paper about 13 centimetres square, and some coloured crayons or felt pens. Use plant shapes for your first design. You could copy one of the shapes on these pages. Make your designs twist and curl to fill the square. Then try an animal or bird pattern to fit another square. Make this design as simple as possible. Draw firm outlines.

Don't worry about making the animal look realistic. You are making a flat pattern, not a picture which looks solid. Colour all your designs with bright colours.

Try to design a pattern that repeats itself. The easiest way to do this is by placing a simple pattern, like the one at the bottom of this page, in each corner of one of your squares. Put several squares of the same design together as one pattern.

Block prints

This frog is a print from a woodcut by the Japanese artist, Hoji.

This Japanese frog is printed from a woodcut. To make a woodcut, an artist draws a design on a smooth piece of wood. He then cuts away all the parts that he wants to be white in his print, and leaves untouched the parts that are going to be dark.

To create a single black line the wood must be cut away from both sides. The bits that are cut out won't catch the ink so they will stay white. Was this frog's mouth cut out of the wood, or left uncut? Hundreds, or even thousands, of prints can be made from one single woodcut before it wears out.

Detailed prints

A woodcut with many fine lines cut into it is called an engraving. This wood engraving of a nightingale was made about 200 years ago. The English artist, Thomas Bewick, made hundreds of woodcuts like this one to illustrate books about birds and animals. He must have been very patient, as all his engravings are tiny and full of details. Blocks for engravings are usually made from box wood, which is hard and lasts for a long time.

This nightingale is a print from an engraving by the English artist, Thomas Bewick.

Cut the vegetable in half so that you have a smooth surface. Leave it to dry for a few minutes. Choose a simple animal shape. Cut this shape out of the smooth surface. You will need to use a sharp knife, so make sure there is an adult to help you. Paint thickly over the cut side of the vegetable, but try not to get any paint into the grooves you have cut out. Then print your shape onto paper.

Make your own prints

You can make a printing block for a simple animal shape. You don't have to use wood — some clear and simple prints can be made by using a vegetable like a potato.

Line drawings of animals

'Elephant' was drawn by the Dutch artist, Rembrandt.

Some of the earliest drawings ever made are pictures of animals. Animals have always been important for food and for work. People have also kept animals in and around their homes for hundreds of years.

A circus animal

Look at this picture of an elephant. With just a few strokes of chalk the Dutch artist, Rembrandt, has drawn the elephant's shape and its wrinkled skin exactly. Look at the way he uses heavy shading to make the animal seem solid and real.

Rembrandt had probably never seen an elephant before. He drew this one when he saw it in a travelling circus in Holland.

Artists sometimes make a whole page of quick drawings of animals to show them in different positions. The famous Italian artist, Leonardo da Vinci, made these sketches of cats – although one of the animals is not a cat at all! He shows us how peaceful cats look when they are curled up asleep, but also how a prowling cat can look as fierce as a lion.

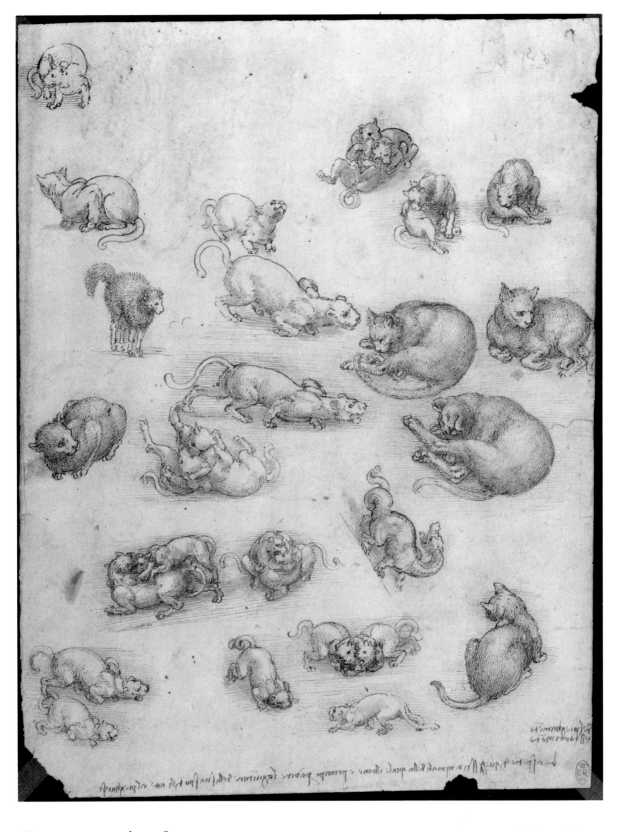

'Sketches of Cats' was drawn by the Italian artist, Leonardo da Vinci.

Draw an animal

Choose an animal that you can study closely. It may be an animal that lives in your house. It could be an animal in a park or a zoo. Draw the outline of the animal you have chosen quickly, without putting in too much detail at first. Notice the way some areas of the animal are in shadow. Shade in these areas on your pictures.

Painting a special animal

'Turkey Cock' was painted by the Indian artist, Mansur.

When we look at an animal portrait we can often tell more about the owner of the animal than about the animal itself. Sometimes people want a picture of an animal they treasure. Sometimes they want a picture to boast about.

A rare bird

This turkey was sent from Portugal as a present to an Indian emperor about 350 years ago. Turkeys were very rare in India at that time. The emperor was so pleased with the turkey that he ordered its picture to be painted! The artist, Mansur, has obviously studied the turkey closely, for he has painted lots of tiny details. We can clearly see the patterns and colours on the bird's glossy feathers.

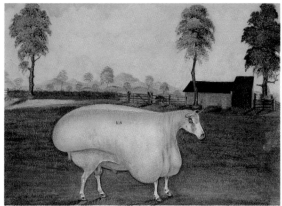

'White Ram' was painted by an unknown English artist.

A huge beast

You probably think this ram looks rather unpleasant, but the farmer who owned this large creature was very proud of it. It's hard to see the shape of the ram's body underneath its enormous fleece. Look at how realistic the background landscape looks compared with the exaggerated figure of the ram.

Make an animal portrait

Choose an animal that is special to you. The ram in the picture was important because it was so fat and had such thick wool. You might choose a dolphin because it is so graceful, or a goat because it gives lots of milk. How can you show these things in a picture? Usually artists make an animal look best by painting it from the side.

You need a sheet of paper, a pencil and some coloured pencils. First draw a frame around the edge of the paper to colour in later. Then draw your special animal from the side as carefully as you can. When your pencil drawing is finished, decorate the frame with a design to match your animal. Now colour your picture. Think about what colours will make your picture as attractive as possible.

Aboriginal bark pictures

The drawings of Aboriginal people in Northern Australia tell us all sorts of things about their life and their history. Their pictures were usually scratched in the bark of trees, or on rocks and the walls of caves.

Aborigines have always hunted animals and fish, and gathered plants and berries for their food. Many of their pictures show animals and hunting scenes. Most of the pictures tell stories. The picture on this page is part of a larger bark painting which tells a story about the birth of one group of Aborigines.

Magic

Sometimes Aborigines drew the insides of an animal as well as its outline. Can you see this in the large picture? The artist wanted to show the inside parts of the animal because they were all important in some way. Some parts were important for food. Others were important because the Aborigines believed they had magical powers.

Make a scratch drawing

You need a sheet of paper, some coloured wax crayons and a thin pointed stick. Cover your paper with several stripes of wax crayon in different colours. Then cover the stripes with a thick layer of one dark colour. Using the stick, scratch a simple animal shape, like the Aboriginal ones, into the dark wax. The colours will show through.

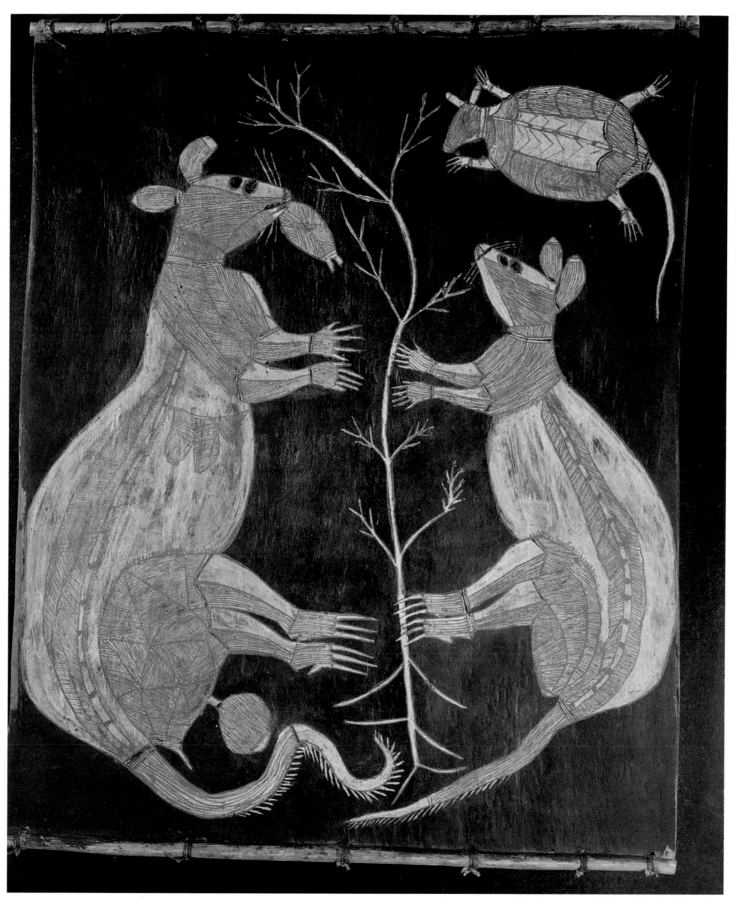

This is an Aborginal bark picture of kangaroos.

Totem poles

A totem pole is a column of wood carved with figures called totems. Each totem has a special meaning. Totem poles are the earliest and best known examples of the art of North American Indians.

The first totems were images of animals which the Indians believed were their ancestors. Most totem figures represent birds, fish or other animals. Some are imaginary beasts from ancient stories. The Indians believed that these images would protect them from harm.

You can only see the front of the totem poles in these pictures, but the back would also be carved. Sometimes the images would be brightly painted. On early totem poles, only important parts like the eyes and ears of the totems were painted.

Types of pole

There were four different kinds of totem pole. Memorial poles were carved to celebrate a special event. House posts were carved poles which formed part of the structure of a building. House-front poles stood against the front of a house, near the entrance. Grave posts were carved poles which supported a box to hold the body of the chief when he died.

This is a North American Indian totem pole.

Important families

Each family in a tribe had its own totems. If you see a tall totem pole, you know that the family who owned it were important. Some totem poles were 27 metres tall!

Your family totem pole

Choose three animals to carve. They could be animals which are important to your family. Try to make your totem pole about 30 centimetres tall.

Find a hard, flat surface where you can work. You will need modelling clay, a knife and a bowl of water. Take a large handful of clay and roll it into a thick cylinder. If the clay is too dry it will crumble, so dip your hands in water.

Stand the cylinder on its end and divide it into three equal sections by scratching rings onto the surface. Then take the knife and carve your animal totems. Remember that your knife is sharp — make sure there is an adult to help you. Try to make your pole look good from the side and back, too! When you are happy with your design, allow it to dry overnight and then paint it.

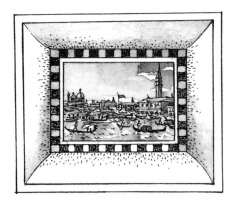

CHAPTER THREE

Places in Art

Artists have different ideas about painting places. In this chapter, you can look at some of those ideas. Some artists followed strict rules about colour and shape. They even made careful measurements to show how places look smaller when you are further away from them. Other artists simply painted places because they loved them and wanted to share their feelings.

Early paintings of a place are never the same as those painted later on. This is because artists discovered new materials and new styles of painting. Also, artists from different countries and cultures will paint places in a totally new way.

You will learn how new discoveries about painting spread throughout the world. Look carefully at the pictures and decide which ones you prefer. Try out the projects and learn how to make models and collages.

The artist's place

The place where artists work is particularly important if they are painting directly from life rather than from their imagination. Some artists have a special place, or studio, where they always work. Perhaps they need a lot of equipment close at hand. Other artists have only a few materials. They can move around easily and choose different places to work.

When you look at the paintings in the pages that follow, you may be able to tell which ones were painted in the country and which were painted in a town. You may also be able to guess which artists

worked inside and which preferred to work in the open air. Many of the artists who paint places took materials with them. They painted places as they saw them. Can you think which images would be easier to paint outside and which could best be painted in a studio?

A Japanese painter at work

The Japanese painter in this picture is kneeling on the floor to work. He is painting a landscape with a long brush. He is probably working from memory, as he doesn't have sketches to follow. He seems to be painting quickly.

The Japanese artist, Ando Hiroshige, painted 'Artist at Work'.

The artist's brushes, paints and water bowl are neatly arranged on the floor beside him. This artist could probably work wherever there is a flat surface to rest on. He does not seem to need a special room for his painting.

Painting in a studio

The picture on this page shows the Dutch artist, Vermeer, painting in his studio. Vermeer has painted a picture of himself at work. Can you see what kind of equipment Vermeer used in his studio? There is a wooden stand called an easel which held the canvas the artist painted on. There is a stool so that the artist could sit at the right height for his canvas. The heavy curtain was probably pulled across a window when Vermeer wanted less daylight to fall on his subject.

Artists like Vermeer always worked in a studio. They sometimes copied models, as in this painting, or worked from sketches made outside. Sometimes they painted from imagination. They carefully prepared their canvases for paint and put the colours onto the canvases in a particular order. Their pictures took a long time to paint — sometimes a year or more.

How do you paint?

Do you sit on the floor and paint quickly like the Japanese artist? Do you paint carefully at a table or an easel like Vermeer? Paint a picture to show the place where you paint.

'The Painter in his Studio' was painted by the Dutch artist, Jan Vermeer.

Special places

'Mount Fuji in Clear Weather' was painted by the Japanese artist, Katsushika Hokusai.

Some people love the sea. Others love the countryside. Your favourite place may be in the heart of a city. Mountains were special to the artists whose pictures you see here. The Japanese artist, Hokusai, and the French artist, Paul Cézanne, both sketched and painted many views of a favourite mountain.

Mount Fuji

In Japan, all mountains are sacred. Mount Fuji is one of the most sacred.

Hokusai drew hundreds of pictures of the mountain. Sometimes Hokusai concentrated on drawing Mount Fuji itself. Sometimes he drew unexpected views, perhaps showing a glimpse of the mountain hidden by a boat or a wave.

In the picture above, Hokusai has painted a pattern of different shapes and colours to draw attention to the mountain itself. The solid red mass of the mountain catches the eye.

Shapes and colours

Paul Cézanne lived near Mont Sainte Victoire in southern France. He studied this mountain again and again, often from different viewpoints. He painted it in watercolour and in oil paints. He sketched it in pencil and charcoal. Like Hokusai, he included details like farmhouses and people in some of his pictures of Mont Sainte Victoire. The picture on the right shows the mountain on its own.

Cézanne was fascinated with shapes and colours. He has painted the shadow on the mountain as a pattern of strong colours. He has used rich, dark greys and blues to make the shadows look as solid as the rocks.

Your favourite place

Choose a place which is special to you in some way. It might be your house or a place where you like to play. Paint a bold, bright picture which really captures the feeling of this place.

Look carefully at the place you have chosen and make some quick pencil drawings. Draw strong, bold outlines of solid objects. Use short, broken lines for the things which seem less important. Make notes about the colours you see.

When you have made several drawings, go home and paint your picture. Copy the shapes from your sketches, and concentrate on strong colours rather than details.

This picture of 'Mont Sainte Victoire' was painted by the French artist, Paul Cézanne.

What is perspective?

The picture on the right is by the Flemish artist, Brueghel. It is so realistic that it could be a view through a window. How did Brueghel manage to do this? He used a technique called perspective. When distance is drawn accurately in a picture, the picture is in perspective.

Foreground

The part of the picture closest to you is called the foreground. You can see plenty of details in the foreground of this picture. The dogs' footprints in the snow are clear. You can even see the dead leaves on the bushes.

Middleground

The central section of a picture is called the middleground. Can you see women gathering sticks for firewood here?

Background

The most distant part of a picture is called the background. Here, you can just see another village across the fields.

This painting by the Flemish artist, Pieter Brueghel, is called 'February' or 'Hunters in the Snow'.

Perspective model

Make a perspective model from three pieces of card. Divide each piece of paper into three sections by ruling faint lines from left to right. On the first piece, draw the images you want in your foreground. On your second piece, draw the middleground on the middle section of the paper. Draw everything smaller than in the foreground.

Then fill in your background on the top of the third piece of card. Now, carefully cut round the top edges of your foreground and middleground pictures. Keeping the bottom edges of the paper lined up, stick the middleground onto the background. Then stick the foreground onto this. Does your picture look realistic?

The vanishing point

'Regatta on the Grand Canal' is one of many paintings of Venice by the Italian artist, Giovanni Antonio Canaletto.

You may have seen paintings where all the lines seem to lead to a dot in the distance. This dot is called the vanishing point. The vanishing point is an important part of perspective.

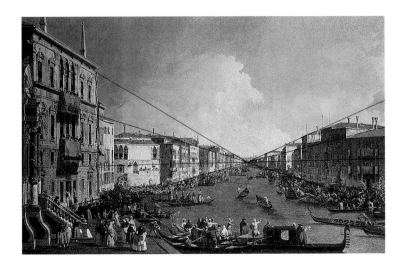

Straight lines

The Italian artist, Canaletto, has used a kind of perspective known as linear perspective in this painting. This means perspective made with lines.

It is easy to tell where the vanishing point is in the picture. If you look at the diagram, you will see how the straight edges of the canal meet at one point in the distance. The lines formed by the buildings on each side of the canal end at the same point. Canaletto's picture is full of carefully planned detail. Every person or boat is drawn to fit in with the rules of size and perspective. He used lines which meet at a vanishing point to create a feeling of space and distance.

A series of bridges

Can you find the vanishing point in this Japanese scene? The artist, Hiroshige, has used the same method of linear perspective as Canaletto. He has also added other details to make us look towards the back of the picture. Look at the bridges in the picture. The bridge in the foreground is in the centre of the painting, but the bridges in the distance are lower down. Your eye follows the bridges to the vanishing point in the background of the painting.

Experiment for yourself

Draw a simple picture using linear perspective. You need a ruler, paper, a pencil and some coloured crayons.

First decide where to mark your vanishing point. Is it to be high or low? Draw a very faint line across your paper, and put a dot to show your vanishing point. Using your ruler, draw 2 lines from this dot to the bottom corners of your paper. These lines will make a road or path. Are you going to have trees or buildings beside this road? Sketch them on your paper, remembering that the tops of the trees or buildings should follow an imaginary line which ends at your vanishing point.

You may need to practise before you get a good result. Take out your pencil and ruler and make lines across your picture whenever you want to check you are getting things right. You can always rub the pencil lines out later.

'Kyo-Bashi Bridge and Take-Gashi' comes from 'One Hundred Views of Edo' by Ando Hiroshige.

Colour and distance

During the 1600s, most European artists used linear perspective to create space and distance. Then they realised that objects could look different in colour when they were farther away. If you look at a tree nearby, you can see every detail of its colour. But a tree in the distance looks pale and details of its colour are less clear. It may seem hazy, as if covered with a light mist. European artists began to paint lighter colours for the background of their pictures to give a feeling of distance. This technique is known as aerial perspective.

Hazy, distant colours

The French artist, Claude Lorraine, worked in Italy and painted large numbers of detailed landscapes. Look at the way Lorraine uses aerial perspective in the painting on this page. Can you see how he changes the colours of distant objects? The foreground is full of dark greens, blacks and blues. The hills and fields in the background are painted in light, hazy blues and yellows to show us how far away the hills are.

The French artist, Claude Lorraine painted 'Landscape with Psyche outside the Palace of Cupid'.

Browns and blues

The Flemish artist, Peter Paul Rubens, also used colour to create distance in the picture on this page. The foreground is painted in rich reds and browns, and the middleground is dark green. The light, bright blue of the distance creates aerial perspective which makes you concentrate on the details at the front of the painting. Can you see any birds in the bushes?

A colour triangle

You can see how aerial perspective works by experimenting with bands of colour. You will need paper and paints, a broad brush and a piece of white paper. First draw a triangle. The bottom edge should be the full width of the paper. The point of the triangle should be in the centre of the top of your paper.

Starting at the lower edge, paint a wide band of dark blue, red or green. Mix a paler shade of the same colour. Then paint another wide stripe above and slightly overlapping your first band, following your triangle shape. Keep mixing the paler shades of your first colour and painting bands until you reach the top of the triangle.

Strength of colour

You can use colour triangles to guide you when you paint a landscape. Make a light pencil sketch before you begin to paint. Put some trees or bushes in the foreground, and remember to make all the details clear. Your background should be hazy. Now look at the colours in the paintings on these pages.

Now make a colour triangle for each of the main colours you can see. When you mix a colour for your landscape, first decide where in the picture you will be using that colour. Then check with the right colour triangle that you have not made your colour too strong or too weak.

'Landscape with Château de Steen' was painted by the Flemish artist, Peter Paul Rubens.

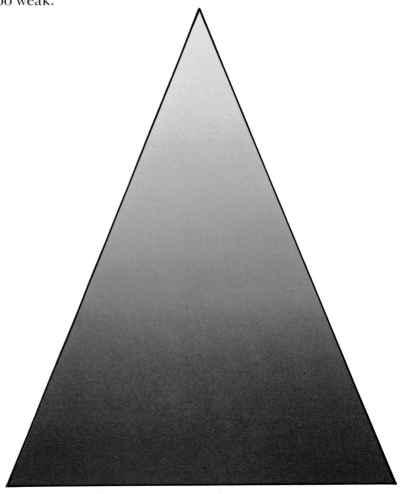

Pictures without perspective

'A Tuscan Town' was painted by the Italian artist, Ambrogio Lorenzetti.

This picture of an Italian town was painted in the 1400s. At that time, Italian artists often painted the same subjects. Paintings of stories from the Christian religion were common and portraits were popular. But a bird's-eye view of a town was thought to be an unusual subject.

The painting looks unusual to us for a different reason. It was painted without perspective! The ground tilts upwards so steeply that there is no room for the sky. The buildings at the back are the same size as the ones at the front. The town is obviously on a steep hill, but there is little feeling that the sea in the background is on a different level.

Early Greek landscapes

We don't know the name of the Greek artist who painted the picture opposite. But we know it was painted around 1500 BC. This huge painting covered one whole wall of a Greek house. Pictures like these are called frescoes. Frescoes are painted onto the wet plaster of a wall. This fresco shows a landscape of hills, plants and birds. Without knowing about the rules of perspective, the artist has tried to give a feeling of distance in his painting. He has drawn the birds in the sky small to make them seem far away.

This is an ancient landscape fresco from Thera, in Greece.

Both sides of the painting are almost exactly the same. The two hills on either side of the central hill are mirror images of each other. The artist has deliberately painted a picture which is flat and balanced. This type of composition is called a symmetrical arrangement.

A balanced picture

You can have fun making symmetrical pictures. You need your brushes and paints and a sheet of white paper.

Fold the paper in half and open it out again so that it has a crease down the middle. Mix some thick paint. First, choose some strong greens and browns. On one side of the crease paint one or two rows of trees. Work quickly so that paint doesn't dry. Now, fold the clean side of the paper over onto the painted side. Press down firmly. When you unfold the paper, the shapes you painted will have printed onto the other side.

A flat picture

'Akbar Entering Surat' is a Mughal miniature painting.

When this Indian picture was painted, artists were respected people in India. They were employed by the emperors to record important events and stories in paintings. These artists painted flat pictures which didn't follow any of the rules of perspective.

Busy scenes

The Indian picture above is a Mughal miniature. The artist concentrated on the colour and details of his scene.

He did not worry about painting distance in a realistic way. The painting shows the Emperor Akbar arriving at the outside gates of an Indian city.

There is so much activity in the painting that it is not immediately clear which figure is the emperor. Is he the man on the elephant at the front, or the man on the black horse? Akbar's black horse is surrounded by other people on horseback, on camels and on foot. The people are all finely dressed in rich, brightly-coloured fabrics. Can you see the musicians dancing as they play?

No shadows

The artist has used rich red, gold and orange colours to capture the heat of an Indian scene. The colours at the back of the picture are not lighter than those at the front. There are no shadows to make any figures in the picture look solid. The town walls are flat, as if they were cut out from cardboard. The artist is telling a story with his picture rather than painting a realistic view.

Realistic flat pictures

During the 1700s, Dutch artists painted flat scenes on the inside of a box and viewers looked in through a peephole. These boxes were called perspective boxes. A well-made box could make a very realistic view. You can make a simple perspective box out of a small box with a lid. Ask an adult to help you cut down all four corners of the box.

Now you will have a flat shape. Leave one short side blank. On the other three sides paint a scene. Paint the base section of the box green. You could glue a twig in the centre of the base to look like a tree. Then paint blue sky on the inside of the lid. You will need to cut a peephole in the middle of the unpainted end of your box. You also need a hole in the lid so that light can shine into the box. Ask an adult to help you cut these holes. Join the sides of the box back together and put the lid on. Hold your box up to a light and look through the peephole.

Playing with perspective

Artists who were familiar with the rules of perspective sometimes played games with it. At first glance, the perspective of the two pictures on these pages seems to be normal. But look again!

'False Perspective' is an engraving by the English artist, William Hogarth.

The fisherman

Look at the sign on the building in this picture. It appears to be behind the trees on the far hill! How could the woman leaning out of the window at the top of the picture light the pipe of the man on the distant hilltop? Can you work out the perspective of the tiled floor where the fisherman is standing? The English artist, Hogarth, has thought carefully about the kind of tricks you can play with perspective. He has deliberately drawn some images in strange positions and other images the wrong size.

An extraordinary building

Now let's look at the drawing by the Dutch artist, Escher, on the opposite page. At first, it looks as if this is a detailed drawing of a house with many staircases. We think the picture is in perspective. But if you look at the picture carefully, you will realise that a building like this could not possibly exist.

Some of the figures going upstairs are upside down. Try turning the book round so that you can look at the picture from a different angle. You might expect the staircases to be the right way up now. But look again. Now another image will be upside down!

Draw a crazy cube

Complicated tricks with perspective like the ones in the pictures on these pages are difficult to draw. The artists spent a long time working out the details in their drawings. You can draw a picture which is easier, but just as crazy! Try copying the 'cube' below. Can you see how its perspective works?

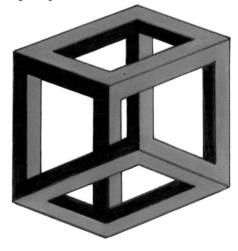

'Going Upstairs' is one of a series of complicated pictures by the Dutch artist, Maurits Cornelius Escher.

Roman trick paintings

This is part of 'The Fall of the Giants', a mural by Giulio Romano.

A large mirror in the far corner of a dark room can make the room feel larger. The reflections in the mirror can look like the view into another room. The Ancient Romans knew all about tricks like this, but they didn't use mirrors. Instead, they painted scenes on the walls of their rooms. These paintings were so realistic that people could imagine that they were not inside a house at all. Today, we call these trick paintings 'trompe l'oeil', from the French words which mean 'deceive the eye'.

Jupiter and the giants

This photograph shows a small part of a huge painting which covered a whole room in a palace in Italy. The artist, Giulio Romano, painted the chief of the Ancient Roman gods, Jupiter, on the ceiling of the room. Jupiter is surrounded by excited followers who are hurling thunderbolts at a group of giants below. Painted columns are tumbling onto the heads of the wild-eyed giants. Walking into this room must have been like walking into the battle!

The seashore in the city

This seashore scene was painted on a wall inside a Pompeiian house. Pompeii was a Roman town which was covered with ash when a volcano called Mount Vesuvius erupted over 2,000 years ago. Beautiful paintings from houses there have been found, but most are incomplete or damaged in some way.

This scene was probably framed by a doorway. Can you imagine the feeling of seeing this pleasant watery view on a wall in your room? You might have felt as though you could have stepped through the door to wave to people on the opposite shore.

Can you see anything strange about the painting? The figures in the background are much larger than those in the foreground! The boat is as small as a toy. But the painting still gives us the calm feeling of a sunny day by the water.

A pretend window

Is there anywhere in your home where you would like to have another window? Perhaps you have a room with a small window, or a window with a gloomy view. You could brighten up the room with a large painted window.

Cut a piece of paper the size and shape of your ideal window. You may need to stick several pieces of paper together. Decide what you would most like to see from your window. Paint this view onto your large piece of paper.

When your painting is dry, frame it with a frame the shape of a window. You can cut a card frame and glue it onto your picture or paint a frame over it. Then hang your picture on the wall. Does it look like a real window?

'Sanctuary by the Sea' is a wall mosaic from Pompeii, Italy.

Painted gardens

'Nebamun's Garden' comes from the tomb of Nebamun in Egypt.

The Ancient Egyptians believed that you could carry your possessions with you when you died. People were buried with food, furniture, clothes — even jewels. The Egyptians also painted the walls of tombs with scenes from the dead person's life. The picture on this page is from the tomb of an Egyptian man called Nebamun. It shows the garden which he loved.

An ancient fishpond

In the middle of the garden there is a pond. Fish and ducks are swimming in the water and lotus flowers are floating on the surface. On three sides of the pond, trees shade the water. We can clearly see what the garden was like, but it has been painted in a strange way. We see the pond from above but we see the plants, ducks and fish from the side. Some of the plants seem to be on their sides. Some are even upside down!

Faded colours

The Egyptians didn't think it was important to paint things as they actually saw them. They always showed things in the way which seemed most clear to them. This painting is more than 3,000 years old, so the colours have faded. But you can still make out traces of bright blues, greens and yellows.

An emperor's wall

The painting opposite was painted on a wall inside a Roman house and is over 2,000 years old. Life-size trees cover the whole wall. Many of these trees are covered with fruit. Painted birds fly in and out of the branches. Stories from the time tell us that the trees were so realistic that live birds used to fly up to the painting and try to peck the fruit with their beaks!

This garden was painted on the wall of the Villa Livia in Ancient Rome.

An Egyptian water garden

Make a paper picture, or collage, in the style of the Ancient Egyptian garden. You will need some old magazines, a large sheet of paper, some scissors and a pot of strong glue. First, make a small sketch to show what you want your finished collage to look like. Use this as a rough guide.

Now paint a pond in the centre of your paper. From your magazines, choose some pictures of plants, fish and birds. Make sure the pictures have clear outlines and bright colours. Cut the pictures out and lay them on your backing sheet.

Look at the picture of Nebamun's garden again. Move your cut-out images about but be careful not to let any pieces overlap. When you are happy with your collage, glue the pictures down carefully.

Light and mood

Choose a particular scene from your neighbourhood and look at it several times during one day. As the sun moves, see how the light changes. Different colours and shadows appear, altering the way the scene looks. Light also changes according to the time of year.

A group of French artists, called the Impressionists, were fascinated by light. One of the most well known of the Impressionists was Claude Monet. When he was a young man, Monet stopped painting in a studio and started to paint all his pictures outside. He concentrated on painting the changes in colour and shape caused by light at different times of the day. He wanted to catch the true effects of daylight on an object.

Monet's garden

One of Monet's favourite places was the water garden at his home in France. He painted many pictures showing a lilypond in the garden at different times. The bridge in this picture was white. But here, the shadows falling on the bridge make it appear green. This is because the light is reflected off the green trees and reeds behind the bridge. The whole picture is a beautiful mixture of greens and purples. Do you think it was painted on a sunny day?

A great cathedral

Monet also painted many pictures of the cathedral at Rouen, in France. Each painting shows the cathedral at a different time of day. In this painting, the colours seem to shine with reflected light. Most of the picture is painted in sunny yellow, but Monet has used darker colours to suggest the heavy doorways, towers and windows of the cathedral. Even though the painting is full of light, we know that this is a strong building.

An impression of a building

One way of copying the Impressionist style is to paint onto wet paper. Choose white paper to help the light shine through your picture. Take your painting materials outside on a sunny day and find a building to paint.

Make a quick pencil sketch of the shape and main features of the building. Then make your paper wet by brushing or sponging water all over it. This will help your colours to flow over the paper. Paint the darker or shadowy parts of the building with darker colours first. Then paint the main part of the building with bright colours. Work fast using small, quick brushstrokes.

'Waterlilies' was painted by the French artist, Claude Monet.

The French artist, Claude Monet, painted 'Rouen Cathedral at Sunset'.

Buildings

'Gare Saint Lazare' was painted by the French artist, Claude Monet.

The best pictures of buildings don't just show us their shape and size. They make us feel as if we are walking around them or even that we are inside the building itself.

A busy train station

Here we are in a busy, working train station. High over our heads is the tall iron and glass roof of the engine shed. Billowing puffs of smoke and steam from the steam engines stand out as light patches against the dark roof. There is movement everywhere.

The painting is by the French artist, Claude Monet. We have already looked at Monet's interest in light. Can you see the effect of the light streaming through the glass roof of the station onto the clouds of steam in this picture? Monet shows us how the shapes of people and engines stood out in the confusion of the smoke and noise of the station. He created the impression of activity by using patches of colour instead of neat outlines. This is such a busy picture that we can almost smell the smoke and hear the bustle of the people!

A forgotten place

This picture has a different feeling. It shows an old ruined chapel where kings and queens of Scotland were once buried. There is no busy activity inside this building. Broken columns stand out against the night sky. They seem to stare down into the roofless building. Dark arches look like eyes watching the empty spaces. Moonlight streams in through the broken roof and windows, and there are patches of black shadow. This building looks lost and forgotten.

Clear details

The chapel has been carefully drawn. We can see every detail of the building as it looked when the picture was painted. Do you feel as if you are standing inside the chapel? The French artist, Louis Daguerre, wanted to paint in the most realistic way possible. Eventually, he gave up painting and became one of the first photographers.

Painting details

You painted a building in the Impressionist style for the activity on page 91.

Now try to paint the same building in a detailed style, like Daguerre's. Before you start painting, make an accurate pencil drawing to follow. Draw in as many details of the building as you can. When your sketch is complete, you can start to paint. Choose a fine pointed brush so that you can paint in all the details on your sketch.

The French artist, Louis Daguerre, painted 'Ruins of Holyrood Chapel'.

The sea

The French artist,
Claude Lorraine,
painted
'A Seaport'.

The sea can be powerful and menacing. You may have seen a rough sea or looked at pictures of shipwrecked boats and stormy waters. But the sea can also be calm and friendly.

What does the sea mean to you? Does it mean playing on sandy beaches? Do you think of boats and travel? Before railways, trucks and aeroplanes were invented, the sea was the most important means of transport. People and goods were taken from country to country by boat. Ships often sank and many people lost their lives.

Calm and secure

The sea does not look dangerous in this view of a port. The towering masts of the big sailing ships and the solid buildings seem calm and secure. Men and women chat on the shoreline as a slight breeze ruffles the water and the flags flutter on the boats.

'Boulogne Sands' was painted by the English artist, Philip Wilson Steer.

On the beach

This scene shows a happy view of the sea. It is a painting of a warm, hazy day on the beach by the English artist, Philip Wilson Steer. There is no feeling of permanence here. It is a picture of one afternoon — perhaps a holiday or a special day out. It may seem strange to you that the children are wearing so many clothes on the beach! The red and white striped objects are huts where people could change when they wanted to swim in the sea.

If you look at the dots and splashes of colour in the painting, you can probably tell when it was painted. Look through this book and see if you can recognise the same style in any other paintings. Wilson Steer greatly admired Claude Monet and the Impressionists, and so he copied their way of painting.

Painting the sea

You don't need to be beside the sea to paint it. You can paint from thoughts and ideas. Make a sketch of some things that make you think of the sea or the beach. It may be sailing boats or rocky pools, or shells like the ones on these pages. Paint your images with splashes of colour and thick, bold brushstrokes.

Choosing a format

Before you start painting, you choose what shape you want your picture to be. Round, square and rectangular shapes are probably the most common. We call a picture's shape its format. The format you choose often affects the way you paint your picture. These two pictures have different formats. The first is taller than it is wide. It suits a tall image, like the

standing figure. This format is called portrait because artists often use it for portraits of people.

If you want to show images surrounding a figure, you might choose a wider format like the second one. This format is called landscape because artists often choose it when they are painting landscapes.

Tall and high

The Chinese hanging scroll on this page uses a portrait format to show a landscape. The tiny people in the foreground contrast with the height of the distant mountains. The tall, narrow format of the picture helps the artist to show the mountains towering over the people below.

This Chinese scroll painting is called 'Visiting a Friend in the Mountains'.

A wide scene

Now look at this painting by the Japanese artist, Gakutei. There is a wide sweep of sea and sky, and the rays of the sun stretch out across the picture. The boats in the background seem very far away. The wide format helps the artist to capture a feeling of space and distance.

Experimenting with format

Look through this book and see how the artists have used format. Think about how the shape of a picture affects the way you feel about the subject. Then try using different formats for yourself. Take a piece of paper with a landscape format and sketch a town. You will have enough room to include buildings, trees and cars. You could even show the surrounding countryside.

The Japanese artist, Yashima Gakutei, painted 'Ships Entering Tempozan Harbour'.

Now paint a town on a piece of paper with a portrait format. You will have less space for buildings and countryside, but you may be able to put in some people in the foreground. Is this picture more crowded than your landscape format?

Let's look at composition

When you pick a bunch of flowers and arrange them in a bowl, you have to decide which colours and shapes will look most attractive together.

An artist preparing to paint a picture has to make the same decisions. The artist chooses the right arrangement of lines, colours and shapes to match the feeling or meaning behind the picture. We call this arrangement composition.

Balance

Look at these sketches. In the first one, the tree is the same size as the house and the picture is balanced. The second sketch looks unbalanced because the tree is larger than the house. Artists often aim to create a balanced composition in their pictures because it is pleasing to the eye.

Shapes and lines

We can use a series of imaginary lines to help us work out how an artist arranges the shapes in a picture. We call these lines composition lines. Look at this painting by the Flemish artist, Brueghel. Can you see the lines made by the trees, the men and the houses on the left? The lines lead you to look towards the back of the picture. This helps Brueghel to tell a story in the picture.

The hunters in the foreground are walking wearily homewards. The people in the middle of the picture haven't seen them yet. But some of them are preparing for the return of the hunters by gathering wood to make the fires to cook a meal. Our eyes automatically follow the composition lines as we 'read' the story the artist is telling us.

Making things look good

Make an attractive composition by pinning pictures to a notice board. If you don't have a board, you can use a thick square of cardboard.

Use pictures cut out from magazines, or a collection of your favourite postcards and photographs. Do you want to make a round composition like this one? Do you want to tell a story with your composition?

Look at the sizes, shapes and colours of the pictures you have chosen. Think where you want spaces between them, and where they could overlap. You may have to move your pictures several times before you're satisfied with your composition and can pin the pictures into place.

'February' or 'Hunters in the Snow' was painted by the Flemish artist, Pieter Brueghel.

Unexpected views

Look at this picture by the French artist, Edouard Manet. It is a close-up view of two people in a boat. But we can't see much of the boat and we can only see part of the woman. We don't know if the boat is on a river or on a lake. You might think Manet has chosen an unusual way to show this scene. But the composition of Manet's painting shows us how it feels to be gliding on the water.

'Boating' was painted by the French artist, Edouard Manet.

Cut-off figures

In Japan, artists had been painting unexpected views like this for a long time. In this print from a woodcut by Kitagawa Utamaro, the head of one of the women is hidden behind a screen. Utamaro shows the scene exactly as he saw it, without worrying about showing the whole of the figure.

'Rolling up the Blinds to Look at Plum Blossom' was painted by the Japanese artist, Kitagawa Utamaro.

Photography

Both Manet and Utamaro have chosen unusual compositions for their paintings. The images in both paintings look almost like photographs we might take today. Photographers can look at objects from unusual angles and capture them immediately on film. Manet was painting in the late 1800s, just as photography was becoming popular. He used composition like a photographer, to paint a passing moment in a realistic way.

Make a viewfinder

If you have a camera you will know how to use the viewfinder to look at scenes from different angles. The viewfinder only shows one part of the scene in front of you. The rest is cut off from sight. The viewfinder inside the camera frames the scene you see.

You can make a simple viewfinder from thin cardboard. Measure four strips of card, 10 centimetres long and 1.5 centimetres wide. Cut these out carefully and stick them together to make a square frame. Then look through some old magazines for pictures of houses or busy streets. Place your viewfinder over the pictures and look at them from different angles.

Do you think the pictures look more interesting if you hide parts of them? What impression do you get if you cut out all the sky? Does it look odd if you hide everybody's heads? Experiment until you find a view of a picture that looks interesting, or amusing. Try to copy this view and then paint it.

Colour and movement

A storm can completely change the way a place looks. A strong wind bends the trees and rain beats down. On a stormy day, even the most familiar place becomes exciting or frightening.

'Landscape' was painted by the French artist, Narcisse Diaz de la Peña.

Storm over a town

Have you ever seen a storm like the one shown in this painting by the French artist, Narcisse Diaz de la Peña? The storm is everywhere. The angry sky is so realistic that it overshadows the town completely. Great patches of light flood down from the sky to light up parts of the hills and the town. Can you imagine yourself in the hills, hiding from the wind and the rain?

Agitated scenery

The style and the colours of the picture opposite are completely different. But there is just as much movement. The wind bends the tall cypress trees and rustles the smaller bushes. The ripe, golden corn ripples in the wind. Curling clouds race across the sky.

The Dutch artist, Vincent van Gogh, painted many outdoor scenes like this one. His thick fluid brushstrokes capture the movement of swirling skies and landscapes simply and successfully. His paintings in this style express a love of nature and a joy in life.

Create a stormy sky

You need some paint and a large sheet of white paper. You are going to paint with your fingers! Look at the first painting and think about a storm. As you think, practise moving your hand to imitate the movement of wind and rain in clouds or trees.

Wet your paper with a sponge dipped in water. This will help you to paint in flowing shapes and patterns.

Put your fingers into some dark coloured paint. Spread the paint in swirling movements across the wet paper, imagining the movement of clouds in a storm. Don't forget to let some white paper show through to add light to your picture.

Work quickly and stop as soon as you are happy with the effect. If you overwork your picture the final result will be too solid to suggest the movement of a storm.

The Dutch artist, Vincent van Gogh, painted 'Cornfield with Cypresses'.

Night light

'Boulevard Montmartre at Night' was painted by the French artist, Camille Pissarro.

Have you ever studied the sky at night? On a clear night in the country the sky is vast, blue-black and covered with thousands of stars. Some stars are just faint spots of light, others sparkle brightly. When the Moon shines, its strange glow lights things up in surprisingly clear detail.

It is never completely dark at night in a town. The orange glow from electric lights means that you can't usually see the stars. But there are many other things to look at. The lights from moving cars cut through the darkness. Lighted windows turn buildings into patterns of light and dark.

Colours in the rain

You can't see the stars in the sky over this city. It is a painting of a rainy night in Paris, France, by the French artist, Camille Pissarro. Light from shop windows, headlights and street lamps shines weakly through the thick rain. The lights are reflected in the wet road and pavement.

Pissarro's blurred brushstrokes give the impression of a view of the street through a wet pane of glass.

Fireworks

The night sky in this painting is lit up by fireworks. The American artist, James Whistler, has painted a firework display on the banks of the River Thames, in England. Fireworks shoot up into the sky like twinkling stars. The bright light of the fireworks means that we can clearly see the masts of the boats and their reflections in the dark water.

Night through your window

You don't have to be outside to make a night-time picture. Pissarro's picture of Paris was probably painted from a window in his studio.

You need a large piece of black paper and your paints. Use the silvery light of the Moon or the golden glow of electric lights as the main focus of your picture. Paint directly onto your paper with bright colours and blurred brushstrokes. Be brave about the way you paint — remember you are just showing the outline of whatever images you can see in the dark!

The American artist, James Whistler, painted 'Nocturne in Black and Gold'.

Modern cities

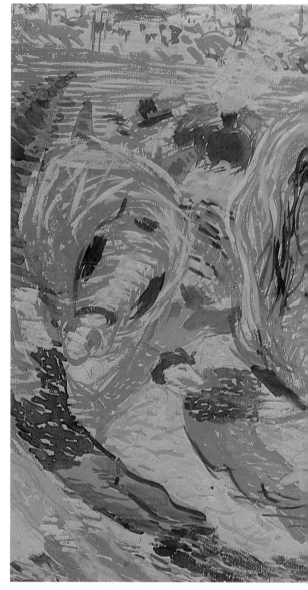

Cities are exciting places. People and cars rush through the streets. There is movement wherever you look! Modern buildings tower above you with tall, dramatic shapes.

Hustle and bustle

Umberto Boccioni was an Italian artist who painted in the early 1900s. He was very aware that the modern world was constantly changing. He was excited by the power of machines. He used strong, bright colours and hard shapes to express the power of city life.

'The Street Enters the House' was painted by the Italian Futurist artist, Umberto Boccioni.

Both these pictures by Boccioni are full of colour and energy. Can you see all the people hard at work in the painting on this page? As the woman leans over her balcony she seems to become a part of the busy city outside her window. In the larger picture, Boccioni has used dramatic brushstrokes to show the power of horses moving through a city. The men seem to be trying to hold the horses still. How do the bold colours in these two paintings make you feel?

Boccioni was the leader of a group of Italian artists called Futurists.

The Italian artist, Umberto Boccioni, painted 'The City Rises'.

They wanted to break away from the traditions of Italian art. The Futurists captured the speed of modern life in their paintings.

Your own Futurist painting

Paint a picture of a street in the Futurist style. Sketch some ideas on paper before you start. Draw a road across the middle of the paper. Put some buildings in the background. Make them strong, square shapes. Then put more buildings along the edge of your road. They could be leaning over, or standing on top of one another to give a crowded feeling.

Your buildings can be all different shapes and sizes, but keep to straight lines and hard angles as you draw. If you show cars or buses in your picture, make them sharp and pointed to give an impression of speed. Remember to use bright, exciting colours when you paint.

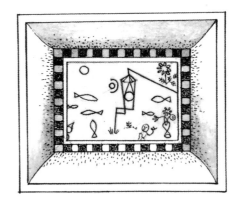

CHAPTER FOUR

Stories in Art

Today, books are so common that we think they have always existed. But books are not old at all! For thousands of years, stories were told through pictures, not words. Some of these pictures were scratched or painted on walls. Others were carved. Sometimes they were embroidered, or drawn on long scrolls.

This chapter shows you ancient and modern pictures which all have one thing in common. Every picture tells a story. You have to look hard to find the stories in some of the pictures. Others are obvious. Many of the pictures are comical. Some of them are bound to surprise you!

There are lots of colourful projects for you to make or paint. You can learn how to paint into plaster, and how to make a simple moving cartoon.

An unknown American artist painted 'Moses Marcy in a Landscape'.

Clues in a picture

There is a story behind every picture you see. Artists use their skills to tell us either about themselves or their subjects in pictures. Some paintings tell their stories in unusual ways that may seem hard to understand. But other paintings are full of clues from the painter to help us understand them.

About the man

This American painting tells us all about a man's life. It is a picture of an American mill owner called Moses Marcy who lived in the 1700s. Let's look at its details to see what kind of man Moses Marcy was. There is a pipe on the table next to him. So we know that Moses Marcy liked to smoked tobacco.

About his work

What can we find out about Moses Marcy's life? The large sailing ship is a clue to his work. Flour from the mill may have been sent to distant places by ship. We can see that Moses Marcy had a grand house, so he was obviously a successful man. Do you think that the book on the table is his accounts book?

Clues about you

How would you tell people about your life in a picture? Write down a list of everything that is important to you.

What do you like best to eat? Where do you live? Do you like sunny days? Do you like to run fast? Do you like reading, cycling or climbing trees?

When you have made a list, take a large sheet of white paper, a pencil and your paints. Sketch a picture which includes everything on your list. Try to make the most attractive arrangement, or composition, you can. Then paint your picture. Use bright colours to make it lively and interesting.

A life story

We have seen how places and objects in a painting can be clues to a person's life. Details like the clothes they wear are clues which can tell us when and where they lived. Occasionally, an artist decides to record so many details in a painting that there is no need for clues. This unusual picture includes every important thing that happened to Sir Henry Unton, a wealthy Englishman who lived in the 1500s.

A busy life

In the middle of the painting is a portrait of Sir Henry Unton. The rest of the picture tells the story of his life. The story starts in the bottom right-hand corner with Henry as a baby. Above this scene is a simple view of the city of Oxford, a university town. If you look carefully you can see a young man studying in a room. This is Sir Henry Unton as a student.

Other countries

After studying at Oxford, Sir Henry Unton travelled to other countries. In the top right of the painting, you can see him in France, Italy, and the Low Countries. This is the old name for modern-day Holland, Belgium and Luxembourg. During this part of his life, Sir Henry was an important soldier. You can see him standing outside a tent, preparing for battle.

Sir Henry Unton returned to England to live the life of a rich country gentleman. You can see him at home in his splendid house where musicians are playing and people are feasting. In the top of this section, Sir Henry is sitting in his study, but he is also at the head of the dining table. On the left, he is performing with other musicians, and below that he is speaking with a group of educated men. Why do you think he is shown doing so many things at one time?

Bad luck in France

Sir Henry returned to France, but he was badly hurt when he fell from his horse. He caught a fever and died.

All this is recorded in the centre of the picture, at the top. Below the death scene, you can see the ship with black sails that took his body back to England. Across the bottom of the painting is a grand funeral procession leading to the church where Sir Henry was buried. Can you see the huge monument that was built in his memory?

A cartoon story of your life

Try making a cartoon to show all the most important things that have happened to you. Start with your birth, and include pictures of yourself at home, at school and playing with friends. Try to join the events together so that it is easy to follow the story.

An unknown English artist painted this picture of Sir Henry Unton.

The story of a year

Do you have a calendar in your home? If you do, it probably has a different picture for each month of the year. The first calendars came from Europe in the 1400s. At that time, most art in Europe was about the Christian religion. Painters were asked to paint pictures to decorate churches, or to tell religious stories. A calendar was part of a prayer book and was known as a Book of Hours. It had a picture for each month or season of the year.

January

This lively picture comes from a French calendar painted for a rich nobleman. The nobleman himself, dressed in blue robes and a fur hat, is sitting at a table spread with delicious food. He is celebrating the coming of the new year with his guests. Outside, knights are fighting a battle and there is a great castle in the distance. The sky is painted in vivid blues and golds. The two symbols in the sky come from a group of twelve signs known as the Zodiac.

October

The other painting is from the same French calendar. It shows farmers sowing corn in fields in front of a magnificent castle. Do you think this is the nobleman's castle? The farmers are busy in the front field but the back one is already sown. It has been covered in nets to stop birds eating the seeds.

'January' is one of a series of paintings called 'Les Très Riches Heures du Duc de Berry'.

These paintings were painted by three Dutch brothers, the Limbourg brothers. The pictures are known as 'Les Très Riches Heures du Duc de Berry'. The Limbourg brothers looked through magnifying glasses to paint the tiny details of each picture.

A special time of year

Is there a special time during the year when you have a celebration? It could be a feast day or a parade. Try to copy the shape and style of the paintings on these pages in a picture of your favourite time of year.

Buildings should go in the background. If you include a group of people paint them near the front of your picture. Use your brightest colours for everybody's clothes, and make the sky a brilliant blue. Draw a semi-circle at the top of your painting and write the name and date of the festival you have drawn inside it in careful handwriting.

'October' is another painting from this series, whose title means 'The Very Rich Hours of the Duke of Berry'.

Celebrations

Styles of painting are always changing. New ideas become popular and old ideas go out of fashion. If you compare an ancient painting with a modern one, they may have little in common. But celebrations have been popular subjects for paintings throughout the ages. Both the paintings on these pages celebrate the birth of a baby.

Noise and colour

This is a painting of a joyful occasion. A peacock is screeching on the roof, a crowd is bustling outside the palace walls, and musicians are crashing cymbals, banging drums and playing trumpets. We can almost hear the noise! There is great excitement because a royal baby has been born.

The picture celebrates the birth of a son to Akbar, a Mughal emperor, who ruled India about 400 years ago. Every detail about the event has been recorded. Each time you look at the picture you will probably find something that you missed before. The complicated patterns and clear, warm colours add to the feeling of excitement.

A feast

The other picture also shows a noisy celebration. The Dutch artist, Jan Steen, has painted a comfortable room where friends and relations crowd around a proud father holding his new-born baby. Food is being prepared for a feast.

This Mughal miniature is called 'Rejoicing at the Birth of Prince Salim'.

Everybody seems to be talking at once! The colours are much softer than those in the Mughal painting. They show the relaxed and happy mood of the event.

A special event

Try to copy the Mughal style of painting in your own picture of a special event. Choose a birthday or a festival. Use a piece of white paper or card no larger than 10 centimetres square. Begin by making a detailed pencil drawing. Put the most important things in the middle of the picture.

'The Christening Feast' was painted by the Dutch artist, Jan Steen.

Make up some decorative patterns and use them to fill in the edges. If you include people, their faces don't have to be very life-like, but do make their clothes as realistic as you can. Colour your picture carefully with bright colours. Take lots of time over your painting. Mughal artists often took months to complete one picture!

Everyday events

The Japanese artist, Kitagawa Utamaro, painted 'Child Upsetting a Goldfish Bowl'.

You have just looked at two detailed pictures telling simple stories. Sometimes pictures seem to be showing a simple event, but can tell us quite complicated stories.

A Japanese child

When Japanese prints and paintings were first seen around the world, people were surprised at how ordinary some of the scenes were. Japanese artists realized that paintings did not have to show grand scenes to be interesting. They painted everyday events as they saw them.

This coloured print shows a woman asleep as her child plays beside her. But it tells us much more. Look at the way the woman is sleeping. It looks as though she has fallen asleep because her restless son has completely worn her out! While she sleeps, he has tipped over the large, green goldfish bowl. For a few moments, he is completely happy gazing at the water splashing onto the floor. The fish are nowhere to be seen! What do you think his mother will say when she wakes up?

A fishing trip

The picture on the opposite page, by the Swedish artist Carl Larsson, shows a family fishing for crayfish. It is obviously not the first time they have been on a trip like this. Everything is well organized! Although they are having a picnic, there is even a table, beautifully spread with china plates and glasses. Can you see the huge pile of crayfish ready to eat? All the members of the family are busy except for one girl, who is sitting waiting patiently for her food.

Carl Larsson painted hundreds of pictures of his family enjoying their country life. If we look at the detail in his simple pictures, we can find out all about life in Sweden at the end of the 1800s. Each of his pictures is like a single photograph from a long movie. They are all part of a larger story.

A common event

When you are at home you probably eat a meal sitting with your family. This won't seem very interesting to you, because you are used to it. But pretend you are a stranger looking at the scene in 100 years' time. You would probably be fascinated by every detail!

What does the room where you eat look like? Do you have shelves on the walls? What do you sit on? What sort of things do you eat? Include all these details in your picture. Try to draw everything to the right scale, and use realistic colours. Perhaps someone will find your picture 100 years from now!

'Crayfishing' was painted by the Swedish artist, Carl Larsson.

Travelling tales

Most people today take travel for granted. Even if we have never travelled away from our own country, we have probably seen pictures and films of distant places. But before machines like trains were invented, travelling was much more difficult.

This English picture was painted more than a 100 years ago, when train travel was a new experience. The artist, William Frith, was fascinated by the stories he saw happening around him at stations. His picture is full of interesting details of travellers at a London station.

A bride and a soldier

A large collection of people are milling around on the busy station platform.

'The Railway Station' was painted by the English artist, William Powell Frith.

Can you see the girls saying goodbye
to the bride in her wedding dress?
A mother is kissing her young son
goodbye while an older boy stands by.
The older boy wants nothing to do with
the scene! A soldier in a splendid red
uniform is joyfully lifting his baby up
into the air. Do you think he has just
come home on the train? He is delighted
to see his child again!

Frith wanted to paint everything that
was happening at the station. He wanted
to record the stories of each group of
people as he saw them. He took over a
year and a half to complete the painting.

The English artist,
JMW Turner
painted 'Rain,
Steam and
Speed'.

Speed

The English artist, JMW Turner, painted
a train in a totally different style. You
would hardly think that he was painting
at the same time as Frith, and in the
same country! Turner was fascinated by
light and colour. He wanted to capture
the speed of a train dashing across
a bridge. The steam from the engine
hides the places on either side as the
train rushes past.

There is a story behind this painting.
A young woman at the time was
travelling on a train in England in 1844,
when she was amazed to see the man
opposite her take off his hat and lean
out of the window. He leaned out for
several minutes, even though it was
raining hard and the train was going
at full speed. The man was Turner.
This dramatic painting was the result
of his first-hand experience of the
train's speed.

Creatures from travellers' stories

Before the invention of modern methods of transport like trains, people travelled the world by boat. These early explorers returned home with stories about the wonderful things they saw.

'The Whale' comes from the Ashmole Bestiary.

But some of their descriptions were so amazing that they were hard to believe. It must have been tempting for the travellers to exaggerate their adventures. Or perhaps the memories of their experiences seemed more marvellous when they reached home!

Bestiaries

Some explorers wrote books describing strange foreign animals that they had seen. The books were called bestiaries. They contained descriptions and drawings of the creatures. The pictures were often drawn by an artist, from a traveller's description. Can you imagine how notes about an unusual animal could become an even stranger picture?

The first place in each bestiary was usually given to the lion. Descriptions of many real and imagined animals followed. Tired eagles were said to get their strength back by flying near the hot sun, then plunging themselves three times into a fountain.

The whale

The sight of a whale confused and frightened many early sailors. A whale resting near the surface of the sea looked so large that some sailors thought it was an island. This painting from an English bestiary records how striking the sight of a whale must have been. It seems to have an enormous number of fins and tails, and its face looks almost human.

The unicorn

This beautiful French tapestry shows an extraordinary beast called a unicorn. A unicorn is an imaginary animal which appears in tales from many countries. It has the head and body of a horse, the legs of a deer and the tail of a lion. Most importantly, it has a single horn in the middle of its forehead. People think that the idea of the unicorn comes from travellers' tales about the rhinoceros!

This French tapestry is called 'Lady and the Unicorn with Lion, Animals and Flowers'.

Drawing a fantastic animal

Ask a friend to describe a strange animal to you. Then take some paper and coloured crayons, and try to make a drawing from their description.

Here is a description of an unusual creature. It has the head of a lizard but the body of a leopard. Its huge eyes are the blue of the deep sea. There are hooves on its back feet but four claws on each front foot. It strides along on its back legs, holding its tail high over its back. Here is a picture of the creature. Would you have drawn it like this?

Stories about dragons

How would you paint a picture of a creature you could never see? Dragons are imaginary creatures, which appear in stories and pictures all over the world. In the East, dragons are seen as powerful creatures who can bring great good fortune as well as bad luck. In Europe, dragons were always described in stories as wicked creatures.

This Chinese embroidered robe was made in the 1800s.

Chinese dragons

According to Chinese stories, the dragon is a magnificent and sacred beast. One description gives it a mane like a lion, horns above its eyes, fins like a fish and a scaly body. It breathes out fire and a pearl rests in the middle of the flames. This dragon can cause rain, wind and storms when it is angry.

Chinese dragons can also bring good fortune. If you look up at the sky during a heavy rainstorm you may catch a glimpse of a dragon. But you can never see the whole of it because it has such a long tail. If you do see the dragon, you will have a long life and great riches. Dragons frequently appear on Chinese porcelain and fabrics, as well as on paintings and scrolls. This marvellous dragon robe was made about 100 years ago for a lady in the Chinese imperial court.

European dragons

The dragon in European stories is always seen as an evil monster. It lives in a dark cave and captures people to eat. A dragon can only be killed if it is blinded. Stories tell us about a brave nobleman who kills the dragon and rescues a captured girl. In most stories, the dragon is killed by a hero called Saint George. You can see Saint George fighting the dragon in this painting by the Italian artist, Paolo Uccello.

'Saint George and the Dragon' was painted by the Italian artist, Paolo Uccello.

Allegories

A picture like Uccello's is sometimes called an allegory. This means that each character in the story has a special meaning. In European stories, the dragon stands for everything that is evil. The girl represents gentleness and innocence. And the fine and noble hero who rescues her is a sign of all that is good. The allegories describe how goodness defeats wickedness through the story of the dragon, the hero and the girl.

Good and bad

Paint a picture showing a dragon that is bad, and one that is good. Which colours would you use for a frightening dragon? Which colours would show gentleness?

A well-known myth

The Flemish artist, Pieter Brueghel, painted 'The Fall of Icarus'.

Some stories about imaginary people or animals are well known in many countries. These stories are called myths. Many of the myths we know today come from Ancient Greek stories.

Daedalus and Icarus

One Ancient Greek myth tells the story of a man called Daedalus and his son Icarus. A Greek king called Minos quarrelled with Daedalus and imprisoned him and his son. Daedalus planned a clever escape. He made two pairs of wings out of feathers held together with wax so that they could fly away. He told Icarus not to fly too near the sun as they escaped over the sea. But Icarus didn't listen. He enjoyed flying so much that he flew higher. Can you guess what happened?

The sun melted the wax, the feathers came unstuck, and Icarus fell out of the sky. If you look carefully at the painting on this page, you can see Icarus falling into the sea.

Many different artists have painted pictures of this myth. This painting is by the Flemish artist, Pieter Brueghel. He doesn't make the story look very exciting! No one seems to be taking much notice of the extraordinary things which are happening. Can you see Icarus' tiny legs? Does it look as though anyone else has noticed them? Brueghel has turned a serious tale into a picture to make us laugh. The little fat legs look quite ridiculous splashing in the sea!

Guessing about the painting

Do the farmers in this painting look at all modern? Have you ever seen a sailing ship like the one here? When you look at a new painting, spend a few moments guessing when it might have been painted. Sometimes you can tell from the way it is painted. Sometimes you can guess because of the clothes people are wearing. This picture was painted in about 1560.

A puzzle of paths

When king Minos imprisoned Daedalus and Icarus, he held them captive inside a maze. A maze is a structure made of a complicated pattern of walls, hedges or paths. There is a picture of a maze on this page. Can you trace a way around the puzzle to reach the centre? You can see mazes in parks and gardens today.

Stories about animals

The Italian artist, Jacopo Bassano, painted 'Animals Entering the Ark'.

Real as well as imaginary animals have been painted and drawn since earliest times. If you look through this book, you will find animals creeping, running or flying on many of the pages! The two pictures on these pages tell stories about large groups of animals.

An ancient story

The Italian artist, Jacopo Bassano, has painted an ancient story. An old man called Noah was warned that there was going to be a great flood that would cover the whole earth. He was told to build a boat to carry one pair of every living creature to save them from drowning. Here, we see Noah and his family shepherding a huge group of animals onto the boat.

Can you recognize all the animals? Bassano painted this picture before 1600. It is not likely that he would have been able to travel to other countries to see wild animals. You may be able to tell which animals he had seen in real life, and which he had only heard about.

A simple style

This picture was painted about 250 years later by an American, Edward Hicks. Hicks worked as a signwriter and he painted in his spare time. His painting illustrates the words of an old story which describes a peaceful world. A lion is eating straw next to an ox, a bear feeds next to a cow and a wolf is lying down next to a lamb. Would this happen in real life? Hicks painted more than 80 versions of this story!

Unlikely friends

Make a cut-out picture, or collage, of a group of animals who might be unlikely friends! You can cut animal shapes out of paper or material, or cut animal pictures out of old magazines. Arrange your animals to make a pleasing picture.

Then glue the shapes onto a piece of white card. Can you think of a title for your collage?

The American artist, Edward Hicks, painted 'The Peaceable Kingdom'.

This crocodile is part of a storytelling scroll from Bengal, in India.

'Gazi Riding on a Tiger' follows the crocodile picture on the scroll.

Storytelling scrolls

Before movies and television were invented, people told each other stories. Storytellers were important people. In some countries, storytellers carried long scroll pictures with them to help them tell their stories. Their pictures were like the very first movies.

An Indian Scroll

In the 1800s, wandering storytellers were common throughout India. These bright pictures are from a fine scroll from Bengal. As the scroll was slowly unfolded, its pictures told the story of the travels of an important holy man.

The scroll is 13 metres long and has 57 separate paintings of different sizes. Lions, tigers, cows and elephants all appear on the scroll. None of the animals look at all fierce. These pictures show a crocodile who was a friend of the holy man. The holy man is also shown riding on a tiger's back. Can you see what he is carrying?

Your own scroll

Think of an exciting story that you have read or heard. Then paint a series of pictures to illustrate it. If you can, paint the pictures on the back of a roll of wallpaper. Or join several sheets of paper together.

Each picture is an important part of the whole story. If the story is dramatic, use colours to match the mood. If there are particular people in the story, try to make them the same in each scene so they can be easily recognized. If the story is amusing, try to put things in your picture that will make people laugh. You may like to work on your scroll with a friend.

When you have finished the main scenes, decorate the edges with brightly coloured patterns. Then use your scroll to tell your friends the story. Have you read a description of the story on the scroll below elsewhere in this book?

Unfolding history

UBI HAROLD: SACRAMENTVM: FECIT: HIC HAROL D:
VVILLELMO DVCI:

'Harold's Oath to William' is a scene from the Bayeux Tapestry.

Tales of dramatic events like battles are passed down through the ages as exciting stories. Artists often choose well-known historical stories as subjects for pictures. This historical story was sewn or embroidered with needles and different coloured threads. This embroidered picture is known as the Bayeux Tapestry. It is 70 metres long and 50 centimetres high. It was made by a group of women about 900 years ago, and tells the story of the French defeating the English in a battle.

Lively pictures

The embroidery is full of life and humour. The part of the story shown above tells how the King of England, King Harold, promises to be loyal to Duke William of Normandy. King Harold looks very miserable.

In the next scene, Harold is returning to England in a longboat. Can you see the man on the balcony looking to see if Harold's ship is near? It is easy to laugh at the simple way the people are shown, but the result is an enjoyable story.

This scene from the Bayeux Tapestry is 'Harold's Return to England'.

A simple moving picture

The Bayeux Tapestry covers the walls of a large room in a special museum in Bayeux, France. When you walk around the room you see the story move quickly from one event to the next. It is almost as if some of the figures are moving!

You can make your own moving picture. Draw the side-view of a simple figure onto the lower right-hand corner of the first page of a notebook. Turn the page, and draw the figure again, changing its position so that it is beginning to walk.

Repeat the process on the next few pages. Copy the figures at the top of this page if you have difficulty drawing your own. Then slowly flick through the pages. Your figure should look as though it is walking.

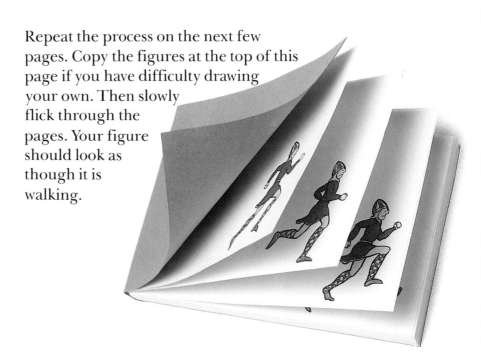

Sculptures that tell stories

Some artists cut shapes and figures out of stone, wood or clay. The solid forms they create are called sculptures. It can take a long time to carve a sculpture, but it is a dramatic way to tell a tale.

Chinese army

Early in the 20th century, some Chinese villagers were digging a well. They were surprised to uncover a life-size pottery figure of a soldier. Can you imagine their astonishment when thousands more figures were uncovered? The figures were all made from a reddish clay called terracotta. They had been buried for more than 2,000 years in the tomb of the first Chinese emperor.

The emperor was a powerful warrior who wanted to be buried with statues of his entire army. The terracotta figures are all life-size. Sculptures of warriors and horses were buried with wooden chariots and real weapons. They were arranged in special positions to tell the story of one of the emperor's battles. No two soldiers are alike.

A storytelling frieze

The sculpture at the top of the next page was carved from a type of stone called alabaster in a palace in Assyria, which is now part of Iraq. The sculpture was made to tell the story of the great battles fought by an Assyrian king called Ashurnasirpal. It forms a long narrow border all round the main rooms in the palace. A border like this is called a frieze.

The Terracotta Warriors come from Xian, in China.

'Soldiers Swimming a Moat to Escape King Ashurnasirpal' was part of a long Assyrian frieze.

In this small scene, three soldiers are trying to escape from their enemies. They must cross a swirling moat to reach safety. One of them has an arrow in his shoulder and another arrow in his side. The other two soldiers are floating on sheepskins full of air because they cannot swim. Can you see them blowing more air into the skins?

Making a frieze

You can make an interesting frieze using modelling clay. First roll out a thin rectangle of clay to make your background. Now decide what kind of figures you will have on your frieze. Perhaps you could try making sculptures of your friends.

Ask an adult to help you cut out your shapes with a knife. Use different colours for each part of your figures. Remember that you can use the end of the knife to make patterns in the clay. Look at the picture to see how to make patterns which look like hair.

Stories on walls

This is a detail from a large mural called 'The Making of Gold and Mosaic Jewellery' by the Mexican artist, Diego Rivera.

The first known pictures were scratched or painted on walls. These pictures were used to pass on historical stories and information. Modern artists sometimes paint huge pictures on the outside of buildings. These pictures are called murals. You may have seen a mural in a town near you.

Mexican murals

The modern Mexican artist, Diego Rivera, realised that mural painting was a powerful way to tell a story. He painted his murals in bright colours on huge city walls so that as many people as possible could see them.

Rivera's stories were about the everyday lives of the people of Mexico. This picture shows part of one of Rivera's murals. These people are all hard at work. They are making gold and silver jewellery. Rivera has painted in great detail to show us each stage of jewellery making from carving to the final decoration. Can you see the fire for melting down the gold and silver?

A Greek mural

Let's look at the other mural on this page. This colourful wall picture was painted by the Greek artist, Theophilos, at the beginning of the 1900s. It tells a simple story about milk. The people in the restaurant at the bottom of the picture are eating fresh yoghurt. The yoghurt is made from the milk of the

'We Have Yoghurt and Sheep's Milk' comes from a wall painting by the Greek artist, Theophilos.

cows and goats we can see at the top of the picture. Theophilos is describing everyday Greek life in his picture.

Painting on wet plaster

Some wall paintings are called frescoes. A fresco is made by painting directly onto the wet plaster of the surface of a wall. As the paint and plaster dry, they combine to make a coloured surface which won't rub off. This is a very old method of painting on walls.

Try fresco painting yourself. Cover a table with newspaper. Mix some plaster and flatten out a small square on the table. It is best to use a small amount of builder's plaster, as modelling plaster dries too fast. Then, with coloured chalk or pencil, quickly sketch the outlines of your pattern. Mix some strongly coloured waterbased paints and paint your picture or pattern as fast as you can. You have to finish the painting before the plaster dries!

Egyptian stories in tombs

'The Weighing of the Heart' comes from the Egyptian 'Book of the Dead of Ani'.

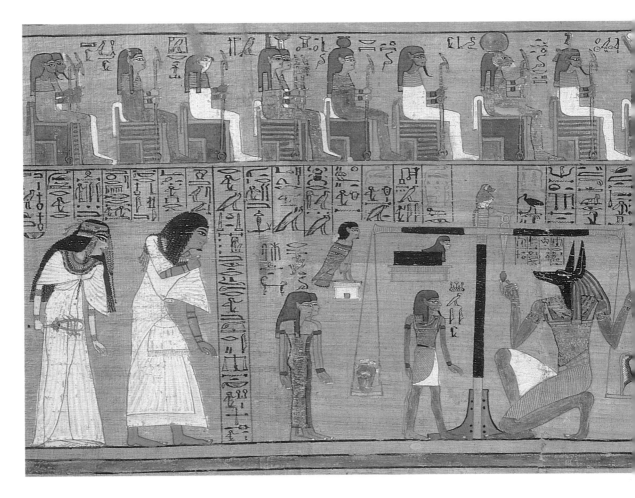

When a story is told in pictures instead of words, we can understand it whatever language we speak. Story pictures from Ancient Egypt have been discovered on the walls of tombs. A tomb is a building which is built to hold the body of a dead person. Many of the facts that we know about life in Ancient Egypt come from these tomb paintings.

A happy new life

The Ancient Egyptians had strong beliefs about what happened to them when they died. They believed that good people went on to a happy new life. Some stories about travels to the next life were painted on a type of paper called papyrus, and placed next to the dead person. Other stories were painted on the walls of the tombs.

A feather and a heart

This story was painted on the walls of a tomb of an Egyptian called Ani. It shows a test which the Egyptians believed a person had to pass after dying. To judge whether they had been good, their heart was weighed against a feather.

This was to get past the four blue baboons you can see in the picture below. The baboons would forgive the person for any small things they might have done wrong during their life. Then they could enter the next life through one of seven gates. As they went through the gate, they were given a cake, a loaf of bread and a jug of beer!

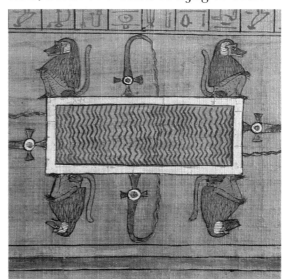

These four baboons also come from the 'Book of the Dead of Ani'.

This feather was the sign for truth. If they had been good the heart and the feather would be the same weight and they could go on to the next life.

In this picture, the scales are being checked by a god with the head of a jackal. A monster is waiting to gobble up the heart if it weighs more than the feather. The two people dressed in white are the dead man, Ani, and his wife.

The four baboons

If the dead person passed the first test, they had to give a special password.

Words in pictures

The Ancient Egyptians wrote in pictures rather than letters and words. This form of writing is called hieroglyphics. You can see some of this picture writing in the paintings. Can you read the message written in hieroglyphs on this page? Some pictures stand for whole words, others stand for letters or for parts of words.

Stories on everyday objects

Look around your home. You may have some paintings hanging on the walls. But can you see interesting pictures anywhere else? Look at the floor. Pictures are often woven on rugs and carpets. Can you also see pictures painted on cups or plates?

Decorated plates and vases

In the 1700s and 1800s, European travellers to China were impressed by the pictures they saw on beautiful old Chinese plates and vases. Some of these traditional designs were changed slightly and copied in Europe. This blue and white design came from China in the 1800s. It tells the story of a young couple in love. They were forbidden by the girl's father to marry. A kind servant helped the girl to escape with the young man. Can you see three tiny figures running across a little bridge beneath a willow tree?

For a while the couple lived safely together in the tiny house. But soon they had to escape further. They swam out to the boat, which took them to the small island. They lived there until the angry father found them. The young man was killed and the unhappy young woman set their house on fire. She died in the flames. But the couple were changed into the pair of blue birds you can see at the top of the plate. And they lived together happily forever.

This willow pattern plate is a copy of a Chinese design.

Persian carpets

This brightly patterned carpet comes from Persia. It was made at the beginning of the 1900s. Rugs are often woven with pictures or patterns which tell stories. Can you work out the story on this carpet? Perhaps it was made for the grand lady we can see in the middle of the picture. Do you think the young man is asking her to marry him?

Make a photograph frame

By making your own frame for a photograph, you can make an ordinary object tell a story. To make the frame, cut a piece of stiff backing card which is 2 centimetres longer and wider than your photograph. You also need 4 strips of white card 3 centimetres wide and the same length as the edges of your backing card.

Stick the four strips carefully onto the edges of backing card, leaving the top edge open. You can slip your photograph in here. With a sharp pencil, draw a design which tells a story about the person in the photograph. Include the food they like to eat or their favourite sport. Colour your pictures in carefully and make the background bright and bold.

This is a Persian picture carpet.

Story pictures from books

'The Foxe and the Raysyns' is a print from a wood engraving by the German artist, Anton Sorg.

Popular stories

In Ancient Greece, a wise man named Aesop made up hundreds of amusing stories about animals. All the creatures behave like humans. The ones that behave badly are always punished, and those that behave well are always rewarded. These kind of stories are called fables. Aesop's fables have been very popular in many countries for a long time.

One of the earliest illustrated books of Aesop's fables was made in the 1500s in Germany. This picture is a wood engraving from the book by Anton Sorg. Because each engraving could be printed hundreds of times, exactly the same pictures could be produced over and over again.

On every page in this book you can look at beautiful pictures in different colours. Thousands of other people will be able to look at other copies of the same book. But this has not always been possible. The earliest books were all handpainted. Each book took so long to paint that usually only one copy was made. In the 1400s, new printing methods meant that many copies of the same picture could be printed at the same time.

An angry fox

The sly fox appears in many of Aesop's fables. In the story picture above, the fox was hungry so he spent a long time trying to reach the delicious grapes above him. Eventually, the angry fox gave up. Aesop told the story to tell us that we can't always get what we want, and that we often don't need it anyway!

A disappointed cockerel

This picture is by the Japanese artist, Kano Tomonobu. It illustrates a French version of one of Aesop's fables. Japanese artists are famous for their fine wood engravings. This engraving was made in 1894, but it copies the style of Japanese prints from the 1600s.

The story shows a cockerel scratching in the farmyard. Among the stones and dirt he finds a precious jewel. Instead of being pleased, the cockerel is disappointed. He was only interested in food and thought the jewel was no use to him. Aesop's fable tells us to be happy with what we are given!

String prints

Make a print to decorate several sheets of paper with the same image. Cover some short lengths of fine string with glue. Then stick them onto one side of a block of wood, curling them round to make the shape you want. For your first try, make the shape of the first letter of your name, and wind a leaf or plant shape around the letter.

When the glue is dry, paint over the surface of the wood block. The paint will stick onto the raised bits of string.

'The Cockerel and the Pearl' was painted by the Japanese artist, Kano Tomonobu.

Press the painted surface onto paper to make a clear print. Why not use your paper to write letters to all your friends.

Unusual stories

You don't have to understand a story completely before you can enjoy it. Some pictures have been painted from stories which are long forgotten. Other paintings tell stories in such an unusual way that we can only guess what they are about.

'The Lion and the Antelope Playing Senet' comes from an Ancient Egyptian storytelling scroll.

Animal people

This picture makes us smile because two animals are acting like human beings. They are sitting on stools playing a board game similar to chess or draughts. The lion looks as though he is wearing glasses. But this is most unlikely because he was painted over 3,000 years ago, long before glasses were invented!

The picture is part of a long Egyptian storytelling scroll where every animal is shown as if it is a real person. We no longer know what stories the pictures originally told.

Dream-like images

Many paintings by the Swiss artist, Paul Klee, show a strange world that is hard to understand. Klee's pictures look like the doodles you might make along the edge of a notebook! It can be hard to remember that Klee was a trained artist who chose to paint in this way.

Klee's fishtank painting might be a scene from an extraordinary dream. In the centre of the picture there is a clock in a net. There are plants, vases of flowers and strange figures. The figure on the right has both sides of her face showing at once. In spite of all this disorder, the fish swim quietly around in their underwater world. They don't seem at all disturbed.

We can be sure that Klee included all the objects here for a reason. See if you can

work out a story that fits the images in the painting. It doesn't matter that your story might be different from the one Klee had in mind.

The Swiss painter, Paul Klee, painted 'Magic Fish'.

Your special picture

Think of some things that are special to you. Or something that you like doing, such as cycling or playing football. You may have a favourite animal, or particularly like one type of plant or flower. How would you show these special things in a painting?

Look at the way Klee has used shapes and colours to make a pattern on paper. Sketch the objects you have chosen on a large piece of white paper. Make sure that you make a pleasing arrangement. When you are happy with the design of your picture, paint it in your favourite colours. Does your picture look anything like Klee's painting?

The story of a painter's life

'Twelve Sunflowers in a Vase' is one of Vincent van Gogh's most famous paintings.

We have looked at the way artists use their pictures to tell stories. We can also use paintings to tell the story of an artist's life. An artist's style often changes several times. These changes in style can tell us about the artist.

Vincent van Gogh

The Dutch artist, Vincent van Gogh, painted over 800 paintings during the last 10 years of his life. They were not appreciated at all when he painted them. Yet they are so popular now that they are bought and sold for huge sums of money. In the 1980s, this picture of sunflowers was sold for so much money that it became the most expensive painting in the world.

Dark and sad

Before he started to paint, van Gogh studied the Christian religion, and spent several years preaching in Belgium. He was not very well suited to this kind of life. He was so unhappy that he fell ill. His brother Theo encouraged him to take up painting. Van Gogh painted the farmers and miners and people he lived with in Belgium. The pictures he painted at this time were dark and sad.

'The Potato Eaters' is an early painting by Vincent van Gogh.

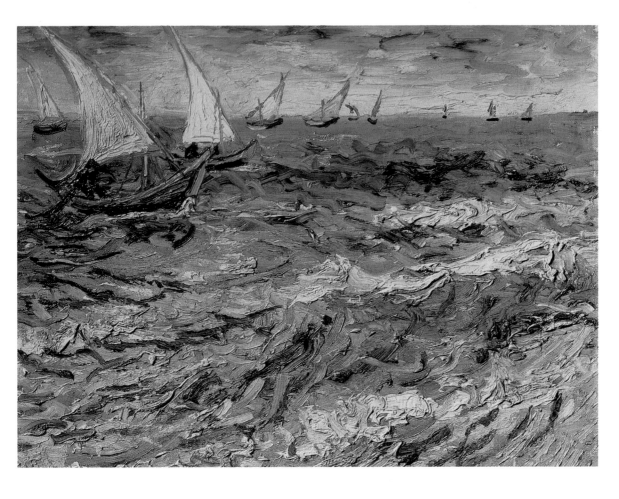

'Seascape at Sainte-Marie' is a view of the Mediterranean Sea by Vincent van Gogh.

Sunshine and colour

In 1886, van Gogh went to Paris to visit his brother. While he was in Paris he saw the colourful pictures of a group of painters called the Impressionists. He was excited by the brightness and joy in these paintings. As a result, his style changed. He moved to southern France in 1888. This picture of the sea is typical of his paintings from this time. It is full of colour and activity.

Unwell and unhappy

But van Gogh was still not happy. In 1889, after a quarrel with the French painter, Paul Gauguin, van Gogh took a razor and cut off part of his own right ear. Soon after, he became seriously ill. In 1890, van Gogh killed himself.

What the pictures tell us

When you know a little about Vincent van Gogh's life, you can look at his pictures differently. Look again at the pictures on these two pages. The dark colours and heavy brushstrokes of 'The Potato Eaters' on the page opposite tell us that this picture was painted while he was living in Belgium. Can you tell when the picture of sunflowers was painted? Do you think he was happy when he painted the self-portrait on the right? It was painted shortly before he died.

'Self-portrait' was painted by Vincent van Gogh a year before he died.

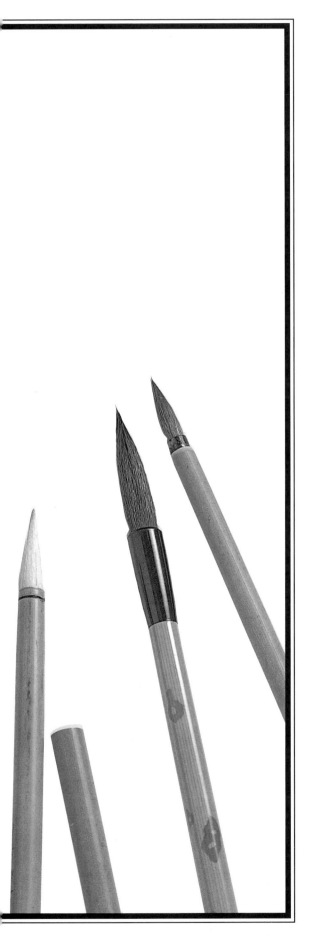

CHAPTER FIVE

Looking at Art and Artists

This book is like an art gallery. Many great works of art and famous artists are now familiar to you. You can stop and look longest at the pictures that interest you most. If you have the opportunity, visit a real gallery. To make the most of your visit, look at the ideas in this chapter before you go.

You have seen the ways artists show people, places, nature and stories. Now you can look more closely at some of these artists. They come from all sorts of backgrounds, and from all different times. And, of course, you are an artist too! You have tried many ways of creating your own art. Have a look at some other materials, and discover easy ways of presenting your own work.

Remember, art is all about you. Your personal ideas and feelings are the most important things. You cannot be told how you should feel about art any more than you can be told how you should feel about yourself. However, your enjoyment will grow if you really take the time to look at art and think about the way pictures are created.

Presenting your own work

Most of the pictures we have looked at in this book are framed and hung on walls. These frames are usually made from wood or plaster, and are often highly decorated. They may be carved, or even covered in gold. It looks very effective if you frame your own work, and there is a very simple way to do this. You need a large sheet of coloured mounting board and some sticky tape,

a metal-edged ruler and a craft knife. The knife needs to be extremely sharp, so make sure there is a grown-up with you when you use it.

Make a simple square frame for your first try. Take the picture that you want to frame, and decide how wide the frame should be. Measure two squares the size of your finished frame.

Using sticky tape, stick your picture in the middle of one of the squares you have cut out. Measure one centimetre in from the edge all round your picture. Mark a shape this size on the other square of board, and cut it out, using the knife against the ruler as before. You will then have a frame.

Put this frame, coloured-side up on to the board with your picture on. Join the two pieces together with a hinge made out of sticky tape. You have now framed your picture.

Mark the squares in pencil on the coloured board. Then place your ruler with the metal edge against your pencil marks. Hold the ruler firmly with one hand. With the other hand, cut along your lines by drawing the blade of the knife against the ruler. Cut slowly and carefully. Don't try and use a ruler without a metal edge because you will probably cut into the ruler instead of cutting clear straight lines in the card.

Art materials

Artists today can choose from a huge variety of materials for their paintings and drawings. There are oil paints, acrylic paints, watercolours and powder paints. Artists can use chalks, pastel colours, pencils, charcoal, felt pens or wax crayons. The thickness of paint brushes ranges from broad to fine.

Some artists paint on a special fabric, called canvas. Canvas is best suited to acrylic or oil paints. There are also many kinds of paper on which to paint or draw. Paper can be thick or thin, smooth or rough, dull or glossy. The choice of paper depends on the kind of picture the artist wants. Pencil sketches look best on smooth paper, but chalks and pastels need a rougher surface. And you can buy a special paper for watercolour painting.

Do you recognize the art materials on these two pages? Which of them have you used? Some famous artists used only one or two types of materials in all their work. Others were equally good at using a range of materials. Try some of the projects in this book more than once, using different kinds of materials. Which work best for you?

How paint is made

Many of the pictures in this book were painted with oil paint. Others were painted with watercolours. Today, we can go to a shop and buy different kinds of paints. Have you ever wondered how artists managed before modern paints were invented?

Early paint

Oil paint was not invented until the 1400s. Before this, most pictures were painted in tempera paint. Tempera paint was made from a mixture of natural colours, or pigments, and egg yolk. Pictures using tempera paint were painted onto a hard, wooden surface. This wooden surface had to be specially prepared for painting. First it was covered with glue and then several layers of liquid plaster, called gesso.

This preparation made sure that the paint would stay on top of the wood rather than sinking in. If the wooden surface was not prepared, the paint would crack.

Look carefully at some early paintings in an art gallery. You will probably be able to see places where the tempera paint has cracked and bubbled.

Watercolours

Watercolours are paints made from pigments dissolved in water. They are much lighter than oil paints. Watercolours fade more easily than other types of paint. Watercolour pictures are painted onto a kind of paper which lets the colour sink in.

Oil paint

Oil paint is made by mixing the pigments with linseed oil and turpentine instead of egg yolk. Linseed oil comes from the crushed seeds of the flax plant. This is the same plant from which linen cloth is made. Turpentine comes from the sap of the pine tree. It is used to make the paint mixture thinner.

Oil paint does not flake and crack as easily as tempera paint. This means that it does not have to be painted onto a hard surface. Instead, artists can paint onto canvases. Canvases are made from fabric. The first canvases were made from linen cloth stretched across wooden frames.

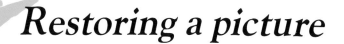

Restoring a picture

Many early paintings were painted on surfaces prepared with gesso. This is a kind of boiled plaster. If the gesso has cracked under the paint, tiny holes appear in the painting. These can fill with dirt. Restorers use fine tools to pick the dirt out of every tiny hole.

Removing extra paint

People have sometimes been upset by naked figures in paintings. So they painted clothes onto the figures! Today, experts use X ray photographs to see how a painting first looked. Then restorers remove any layers of paint that don't belong to the original painting.

Replacing the backing

Sometimes the back of a painting needs restoring. The first oil paintings were painted onto linen cloth. Over the years, the cloth weakens and eventually can no longer support the paint. Clever restorers can replace the backing, leaving the painting intact. They carefully scrape away the old cloth. Then they join the old painting to a new canvas lining with hot wax. They do this on a special heated table. Old paintings can gradually fall into a poor condition. They become covered with dirt from the air. Paint tends to crack, and colours may fade or darken. There are specialists who know about the old methods of painting. They can bring paintings back to their original condition. We call this process restoring a painting. All restoration work takes a long time and a great deal of skill.

Varnish

Most paintings are covered with a light varnish to protect them. Varnish may turn brown and crack or blister as it ages. The first stage in restoring a painting is to remove the old varnish. To do this, skilled restorers use tiny pieces of soft material such as cotton wool, dipped in a special liquid, like alcohol. The cotton wool is rubbed gently over the surface of the painting. The alcohol dissolves the varnish and is mopped up by the cotton wool. This work must be done slowly and carefully so that the paint below the varnish is not dissolved as well.

Cleaning the painting

Once the varnish is removed the paint can be cleaned. Paintings may be in poor condition because the backing board or canvas has become damaged. Or because the varnish has cracked or become discoloured. If the backing of the painting was not prepared properly, the paint may have flaked or cracked.

Visiting a gallery

Gallery rules

All art galleries have certain rules. Usually, the most important rule is that you mustn't touch the exhibits. You will often find a security guard in each room of a gallery. They are there to protect the works of art. Sometimes guards start worrying if people get too close!

Behind the scenes

Many large art galleries employ hundreds of people to make sure that exhibits are well cared for and attractively displayed. Curators have special knowledge about particular works of art. Restorers clean and repair pictures and sculptures. Bright light may damage paintings and sculptures, and damp surroundings are very bad for pictures. Scientists make sure that all the works of art are kept in suitable conditions. There may also be gallery photographers, frame makers, exhibition organizers and teachers. Can you think who else might be needed?

Visiting an art gallery

When you arrive, look for a noticeboard somewhere near the entrance. There will be lots of interesting information here. You can find out how big the gallery is. You can also check what special exhibitions are on show. Does the gallery just have paintings, or are there sculptures, drawings and prints as well? Each piece of art is called an exhibit. See if the exhibits come from all over the world or whether they are all from one country. Does the gallery contain works by living artists, or not?

Whatever else you do, don't try to look at everything. You will enjoy your visit much more if you concentrate on a few things. Think about what you are looking at, and ask yourself questions. Remember, you don't have to like everything. Most art galleries label the things on show. These labels usually tell you the name of the artist and the date and title of the work of art. The other information is usually just for the gallery's records.

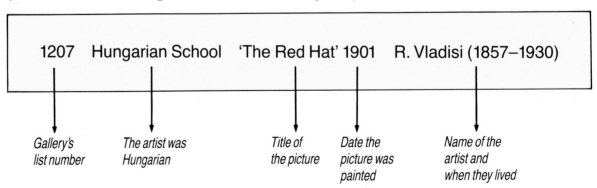

1207 Hungarian School 'The Red Hat' 1901 R. Vladisi (1857–1930)

Gallery's list number

The artist was Hungarian

Title of the picture

Date the picture was painted

Name of the artist and when they lived

More information

Galleries usually sell books or catalogues which tell you all about their collection of art. These are very useful if you see something which particularly interests you and want to find out more. Unfortunately, they are almost always written for adults.

There are art galleries in many of the world's towns and cities. A gallery may be a building all on its own or it may be part of a museum. Art galleries are usually free, but sometimes you have to pay an entrance fee. Some galleries encourage children to visit by putting on special projects for them. Ask about this when you go and look around.

When the artists lived

This chart tells you the dates for all the artists talked about in this book. The artists are grouped into centuries, according to the year of their birth. The centuries are coloured, starting with pink for ancient times, orange for the 1200s and ending with purple for the 1900s.

Cave painters	Jacopo Bassano 1510–1592
	Anthony van Dyck 1599–1641
Ancient Egyptian artists	Pieter Brueghel c.1515–1569
de Limbourgs –1416	Claude Lorraine 1600–1682
Ancient Roman artists	Giuseppe Arcimboldi 1527–1593
Jan van Eyck –1441	Rembrandt van Rijn 1606–1669
Duccio di Buoninsegna 1260–1318	Sayyid Ali c.1546–1600
Paolo Uccello 1396–1475	Jan Steen 1626–1679
Ambrogio Lorenzetti c.1290–1348	Mansur –c.1600
Leonardo da Vinci 1452–1519	Jan Vermeer 1632–1675
Abul Hasan –c.1600	
Albrecht Dürer 1471–1528	Jan van Huysum 1682–1749
Nicholas Hilliard 1547–1619	
Raphael 1483–1520	William Hogarth 1697–1764
Isaac Oliver c.1565–1617	
	Giovanni Canaletto 1697–1768
Peter Paul Rubens 1577–1640	

Matsumato Hoji   c.1740–1800

Louis Daguerre   1787–1851

Joseph Wright   1743–1797   William Morris   1834–1896

Ammi Phillips   1788–1865   Edvard Munch   1863–1944

Thomas Bewick   1753–1828   Paul Cézanne   1839–1906

Ando Hiroshige   1797–1858   Henri Matisse   1869–1954

Kitagawa Utamaro   1754–1806   William de Morgan   1839–1917

Utagawa Kuniyoshi   1797–1861   Paul Klee   1879–1940

Katsushika Hokusai   1760–1849   Claude Monet   1840–1926

Narcisse Diaz de la Peña   1808–1876   Umberto Boccioni   1882–1916

Kitao Masayoshi   1761–1824   Auguste Renoir   1841–1919

Honoré Daumier   1808–1879   Diego Rivera   1886–1957

Caspar-David Friedrich   1774–1840   Henri Rousseau   1844–1910

William Powell Frith   1819–1909   Maurits Escher   1898–1972

J M W Turner   1775–1851   Paul Gauguin   1848–1903

Camille Pissarro   1830–1903   Henry Moore   1898–1986

John Constable   1776–1837   Vincent van Gogh   1853–1890

Edouard Manet   1832–1883

Edward Hicks   1780–1849   Carl Larsson   1855–1919

James Whistler   1834–1903

John James Audubon   1785–1851   Georges Seurat   1859–1891

Edgar Degas   1834–1917

Yashima Gakutei   1786–1868   Philip Wilson Steer   1860–1942

Artists' biographies

A biography is the history of a person's life. These short biographies will help you to find out more about some of the artists mentioned in this book.

Sayyid Ali (c.1546–1600)

Sayyid Ali was a celebrated Persian painter. He is well known for his skill in painting miniature pictures. His major work was illustrating the story of the adventurer, Hamza, for the Indian emperor, Akbar. This story was told in 12 books containing over 1,000 illustrations. Sayyid Ali was in charge of a team of 100 painters, gilders and bookbinders, and the work took 15 years to complete.

Giuseppe Arcimboldi (1527–1593)

Arcimboldi came from Milan, in Italy. His best-known paintings are strange portraits made out of fruit, flowers and vegetables. He painted many of these fantastic faces for the Hapsburg ruler, Rudolf. About 300 years after his death a group of painters, known as the Surrealists, were inspired by Arcimboldi to paint ordinary objects in bizarre and peculiar ways.

Jacopo Bassano (1510–1592)

The Italian painter, Jacopo Bassano, was the father of a family of painters. They all worked together in one studio. At the time, most paintings in Italy showed religious or historical stories. The Bassano family were some of the first painters to make the animals and scenery in a painting more important than the story behind the picture.

Umberto Boccioni (1882–1916)

The Italian artist, Umberto Boccioni, was fascinated by the modern world. As a young man, he painted realistic pictures. Later, he became the leader of a group of artists who believed that Italian art had been following the same traditions for too long. This group was called the Futurists. The name explained their interest in the future and their break away from the past. Boccioni's paintings began to use bolder colours and brushstrokes, and his pictures became less realistic. Boccioni was killed when he fell from a horse at the age of 34.

Pieter Brueghel (the Elder) (c.1525–1569)

Pieter Brueghel was born in the Netherlands. We don't know much about his life except that he visited Italy and France. He is called 'the Elder' because his son was also called Pieter. He is sometimes known as Peasant

Brueghel. Brueghel actually lived in a town but most of his pictures show simple village people at work and play. Some of his paintings are funny, and most are full of energy. They leave a vivid record of peasant life in the 1500s.

Paul Cézanne (1839–1906)

As a young man the French artist, Paul Cézanne, was a member of the group of painters known as the Impressionists. Cézanne was an organized person, and he began to find the Impressionists' style too messy. Instead of copying an earlier style, Cézanne decided to start painting again as if he was the first painter in the world. He wanted to paint objects as firm, solid forms, at the same time as painting light and colour. Cézanne lived in the south of France and devoted his whole life to painting. His clever use of shape and colour came to be greatly admired. The Spanish painter, Pablo Picasso, followed many of Cézanne's ideas. Picasso became the most famous painter of the 1900s.

Leonardo da Vinci (1452–1519)

Leonardo da Vinci lived in Italy at the beginning of a time of great changes. People were starting to recognize the importance of art, architecture, science and literature. This period is called the Renaissance. Leonardo was a talented engineer, scientist and mathematician, as well as a painter, sculptor and architect. He studied the science of the human body and was the first painter to show people with realistic expressions in accurate positions. His best-known painting, the 'Mona Lisa', hangs in the Louvre, a famous art gallery and museum in Paris.

Albrecht Dürer (1471–1528)

The German artist, Albrecht Dürer, was a painter, engraver and stained glass maker. He was also a jeweller. When he was only 13, he drew a skilled portrait of himself. This is recognized as the first European self-portrait. Dürer studied people and nature very closely and made thousands of drawings, paintings and engravings of what he saw. Many people think that Dürer is the one of the most talented artists who have ever lived.

Maurits Cornelius Escher (1898–1972)

The Dutchman, Maurits Cornelius Escher, specialised in extraordinary drawings. He created hundreds of very similar pictures which are interesting because they are all so complicated. His staircases and waterfalls seem to go up at the same time as they go down. At first glance, his buildings look realistic. But when you look closely, nothing is as it seems. Escher's drawings are based on his knowledge of mathematics and architecture.

Edward Hicks (1780–1849)

The American artist, Edward Hicks, was a signpainter by trade. He was a deeply Christian man, and a part-time preacher. Painting was his hobby, and he painted hundreds of simple pictures. These paintings illustrate his beliefs about the importance of peace in the world. There were many painters like Hicks in America in the 1700s and 1800s. They are known as folk artists, or naive painters. They were artists who had never studied art. They all painted in a simple style.

82

Katsushika Hokusai (1760–1849)

The Japanese artist, Hokusai, made an astonishing number of drawings, prints and paintings. From the age of six, he spent most of his time drawing. By the time he was 50, he had produced more pictures and designs than anybody could count. But he didn't paint or draw any of his famous pictures until he was over 65! His life was very disorganized. He changed his name 50 times. He moved house 93 times. He moved when his house became too dirty to clean up! He was always poor.

Paul Klee (1879–1940)

Paul Klee was a Swiss painter who described his paintings as "taking a line for a walk". His pictures are painted in a strange, simple style. He loved all kinds of art as a child, and was very good at playing the violin. He was a brilliant art teacher and taught for many years at the German Bauhaus. This was a famous college that tried to show how art was important in everyday life. Klee was one of a group of artists who were known as The Blue Rider group.

The Limbourg brothers (died c.1416)

Jean, Herman and Pol de Limbourg came from the Netherlands. They were famous as brilliant illustrators. As teenagers they worked for a goldsmith in Paris. This was important training for their work on detailed miniature paintings. But this work for a rich man also caused some trouble. At one time the brothers were imprisoned by a

greedy nobleman in Brussels until a ransom was paid to set them free. The Limbourgs were employed by rich French noblemen. It is believed that they died from an outbreak of the plague in about 1415.

Claude Lorraine (1600–1682)

Claude Lorraine was born in France, but worked mainly in Italy. He is sometimes known as Claude Gelée, or just as Claude. He first trained as a pastry cook, but he became the most famous landscape painter of the 1600s. All his paintings seem rather similar to us today, but in the 1600s his ideas were completely new. Even when he was alive his paintings were popular and very expensive. They were often copied by other artists who tried to sell their imitations as real Claude paintings.

Henri Matisse (1869–1954)

The modern French artist, Henri Matisse, studied law before turning to painting. His pictures are full of decorative patterns of lines and colours. At the beginning of the 1900s, Matisse was the leader of a group of young painters who were known as Les Fauves. This means The Wild Things. They were called this because of the way they enjoyed bright, powerful colours. They weren't interested in copying shapes from nature. Instead, they turned everything they saw into flat patterns. This style has influenced many modern painters.

Claude Monet (1840–1926)

The first successful pictures drawn by the French artist, Claude Monet, were cartoons and funny sketches. These were instantly popular. But Monet's style changed as he became fascinated by painting light and nature. He became the leader of the group of painters known as the Impressionists. Monet's life was not easy. He was very poor and his first wife was ill for many years. Many of his most beautiful paintings show places in the garden he created for himself and his wife. Monet began to go blind in 1908 but he continued to paint at home in his garden. His paintings became popular shortly before he died.

a group of painters known as the Expressionists. Expressionists believed that art should express real feelings, even if the feelings were unpleasant or unhappy. This was very different from the way most people thought about art at the time Munch was painting. Munch travelled all over the world and made thousands of paintings and woodcuts. These pictures did not become popular until he was a very old man.

Pablo Picasso (1881–1973)

Picasso is often thought of as the most original artist of the 1900s. He was born in Màlaga, in Spain, but spent much of his life in France. Between 1901 and 1904, Picasso painted many pictures in shades of blue. This time is now known as his Blue Period. Then came his Rose Period, when he painted pictures in shades of pink. Later, Picasso painted his most famous pictures. They are full of jagged, overlapping shapes and sharp edges. This style became known as Cubism. Picasso is also well known for his sculpture.

Henry Moore (1898–1986)

Henry Moore is one of Britain's best-known sculptors. Moore started making a sculpture by looking at the stone or wood and finding out what shape it suggested to him. He first became famous in 1948 when he won an important international sculpture competition in Venice. His sculptures are usually large and many can be seen outside, in parks or at entrances to buildings.

Edvard Munch (1863–1944)

The Norwegian painter, Edvard Munch, had an important influence on the art of this century. He was the first member of

Rembrandt van Rijn (1606–1669)

The Dutch artist, Rembrandt, painted over 600 paintings during his life, and made more than 1,000 drawings and hundreds of etchings. We have a good record of how Rembrandt looked during his life, as he painted more than 70 self-portraits. He was popular and successful when he was young, but in his old age he was sad and poor. Rembrandt is best known for his drawings and paintings of people. His other well-known pictures show stories about religion. Rembrandt also made some very realistic drawings of animals.

Henri Rousseau (1844–1910)

Henri Rousseau was a French customs officer whose favourite hobby was painting. He is sometimes known as Le Douanier, or the Customs Man. He eventually gave up his job to paint full time. He painted exotic animals and tropical scenery, although he had probably never been out of France. He used plain colours and clear outlines, and his paintings are very simple. This style of painting is called naive. Naive painters have never been trained as artists.

Auguste Renoir (1841–1919)

The French artist, Renoir, studied painting with several other painters who became known as the Impressionists. Renoir liked to paint lively groups of figures. He usually used the maids in his house as models. Renoir's pictures were full of sketchy patches of colour and contrasts of light and shade. Because there wasn't much realistic detail in his paintings, people at the time often thought his pictures were careless and unfinished. Renoir painted more than 6,000 paintings. Even when he became crippled in old age, he carried on painting by wedging brushes between his twisted fingers.

Peter Paul Rubens (1577–1640)

The Flemish painter, Peter Paul Rubens, was famous all over Europe during his lifetime. Born in Antwerp, he spent several years studying art in Spain and Italy. He was a talented and energetic painter. He could paint huge landscapes as well as portraits. Rubens was popular with the European rulers of the time, and was employed by them as a travelling politician as well as a painter. He worked with various assistants and produced an enormous amount of work.

Jan Steen (1626–1679)

The Dutch painter, Jan Steen, was born in Leiden in Holland. He is well known as a painter of humorous, everyday scenes. His crowded colourful pictures often show people of all ages laughing, eating or dancing. Some of the people he painted were figures from the Dutch popular theatre of the time. Steen also painted works based on proverbs and stories from the Christian religion.

Joseph Mallord William Turner (1775–1851)

The English painter, JMW Turner, was the son of a London barber. He began to earn his living by painting scenes of churches and towns when he was only 13. These pictures were popular. Turner's style changed as he became more and more fascinated by light and movement in nature. The pictures we know best are full of swirling colour and light. These paintings were so different from ones painted by other artists of his time that even his friends thought he was mad! When Turner was an old man he refused to show anybody his paintings because no one really appreciated them.

Paolo Uccello (1396–1475)

Paolo Uccello was an Italian painter who lived for a long time but painted very little. Uccello was fascinated with new ideas about space and perspective. He was one of the first painters to try to make his figures look solid. As a result, all his paintings of horses look like carved toy horses rather than real creatures. It is said that perspective was the most important thing in Uccello's life. His fellow artists thought that he was completely mad!

Kitagawa Utamaro (1753–1806)

Kitagawa Utamaro was a leading Japanese printmaker. At the start of his career in Tokyo, he concentrated on nature studies and published many illustrated books. In about 1791, he turned to making portraits of beautiful women. He often painted women from the waist up, to capture their elegant hands, faces and hairstyles.

Index

The publishers would like to thank the following for permission to reproduce these works of art:

Cave painting of hunters; 'Hunting Fowl in the Marshes', from the Tomb of Nebamun; 'Vertumnus' by Giuseppe Arcimboldi; Yoruba ritual mask; 'Fish mosaic from the 1st Century AD'; 'Dreaming', Aboriginal painting; 'Sanctuary by the Sea', a Pompeiian Mosaic; 'Lady and the Unicorn with Lion, Animals and Flowers', French tapestry; 'We have Yoghurt and Sheep's Milk' by Theophilos, 1873-1934; all by courtesy of the Ancient Art & Architecture Collection, London, UK. 'A Tuscan Town' ('Veduta di una città') by Ambrogio Lorenzetti; 'The Fall of the Giants' ('Sala dei Gigante Parete eou Gigante e coloure'); 'The Garden of the Villa Livia' all by courtesy of Archivi Alinari, Florence, Italy. 'Portrait of a young man' by Raphael, by courtesy of the Ashmolean Museum, Oxford, UK. 'The Whale' from the Ashmole Bestiary, by courtesy of the Bodleian Library, Oxford, UK. 'Going Upstairs' a lithograph by Maurits Cornelius Escher, by courtesy of Museum Boymans van Beunigen, Rotterdam, Holland. 'The Children's Afternoon at Wargemont' by Auguste Renoir, 1884, by courtesy of Bildarchiv Preussicher Kulturbesitz, Berlin, Germany. Self-portrait by Rembrandt, 1606-1669, in Kenwood House, London, UK; 'The Orrery' by Joseph Wright, 1734-1797, in Derby Museum and Art Gallery, Derby, UK; 'Sunday Afternoon on the Işle of the Grande Jatte' by Georges Seurat, 1859-1891, from the Art Institute of Chicago, USA; 'The Scream' by Edvard Munch, 1863-1944, from Nasjonalgalleriet, Oslo, Norway; 'Woman Weeping' by Pablo Picasso, 1881–1973, in a private collection, © DACS 1991; 'Portrait of Mariana of Austria, Queen of Spain' by Diego Rodriguez de Silva y Velasquez, 1599–1660, in the Prado, Madrid, Spain; 'Girl in a red dress' by Ammi Phillips, 1788-1865, in a private collection; 'Portrait of a Young Man' by Nicholas Hilliard, 1547-1619, in the Victoria & Albert Museum, London, UK; 'Children's Games' by Pieter Brueghel the Elder, c.1515-1569, in the Kunsthistorisches Museum, Vienna, Austria; 'Still life with fruit and flowers' by Jan van Huysum, 1682-1749, in the National Gallery, London, UK; 'Fire at Sea' by JMW Turner, 1775-1851, in the Tate Gallery, London, UK; 'The Wreck of The Hope' by Caspar-David Friedrich, 1774-1840, in the Kunsthalle, Hamburg, Germany; 'The Allotments' by Vincent van Gogh, 1853-1890, in a private collection; 'The Hare' by Albrecht Dürer, 1471-1528, from the Albertina Graphic Collection, Vienna, Austria; 'View of Salisbury Cathedral from the Bishop's Grounds' by John Constable, 1776-1837, in the Victoria & Albert Museum, London, UK; 'Park near L' by Paul Klee, 1879-1940, in the Kunstmuseum, Bern, Switzerland; 'Nightingale' by Thomas Bewick, 1753-1828, owned by the Folio Society, London, UK; 'The Painter in his Studio' by Jan Vermeer, 1632-1675, in the Kunsthistorisches Museum, Vienna, Austria; 'Fuji in Clear Weather' by Katsushika Hokusai, 1760-1849, in the British Museum, London, UK; 'Mont Sainte Victoire' by Paul Cézanne, 1838-1906, in the Buhrle Foundation, Zurich, Switzerland; 'Hunters in the Snow - February' by Pieter Breughel the Elder, 1515-69, in the Kunsthistorisches Museum, Vienna, Austria; 'Regatta on the Grand Canal' by Giovanni Antonio Canaletto, 1697-1768, in Bowes Museum, Co. Durham, UK; 'Landscape with Château de Steen' by Peter Paul Rubens, 1577-1640, in the National Gallery, London, UK; 'Boating' by Edouard Manet, 1832-1883, in the Metropolitan Museum of Art, New York, USA; 'Waterlilies' by Claude Monet, 1840-1926, in the National Gallery, London, UK; 'Rouen Cathedral at Sunset' by Claude Monet, 1840-1926, in the Pushkin Museum, Moscow, USSR; 'Gare Saint Lazare' by Claude Monet, 1840-1926, in the Musée Orsay, Paris, France; 'Cornfield with Cypresses' by Vincent van Gogh, 1835-1890, in the National Gallery, London, UK; 'Boulevard Montmartre at Night' by Camille Pissarro, 1831-1903, in the National Gallery, London, UK; 'Nocturne in Black and Gold' by James Abbott McNeill Whistler, 1834-1903, in the Tate Gallery, London, UK; 'The Street Enters the House' by Umberto Boccioni, 1882-1916, in the Niedersachsische Landesmuseum, Hanover, Germany; 'The City Rises' by Umberto Boccioni, in the Collection Jesi, Milan, Italy; 'Crayfishing' by Carl Larsson, 1855-1919, in the National Museum, Stockholm, Sweden; 'The Railway Station' by William Powell Frith, 1819-1909, in the Royal Holloway and Bedford New College, Egham, Surrey, UK; 'Rain, Steam and Speed' by JMW Turner, 1775-1851, in the National Gallery, London, UK; 'Saint George and the Dragon' by Paolo Uccello, 1397-1475, in the National Gallery, London, UK; 'Fall of Icarus' by Pieter Brueghel the Elder, c.1515-1569, in the Musée Royaux des Beaux-Arts de Belgique, Brussels, Belgium; 'Animals Entering the Ark' by Jacopo Bassano, c.1510-1592, in the Prado, Madrid, Spain; 'The Peaceable Kingdom' by Edward Hicks, 1780-1849, in the Philadephia Museum of Art, Pennsylvania, USA; 'The Making of Gold and Mosaic Jewellery' by Diego Rivera, 1886-1957, in The National Palace, Mexico; 'Magic Fish' by Paul Klee, 1879-1940, in the Philadelphia Museum of Art, Pennsylvania, USA; 'The Potato Eaters' by Vincent van Gogh, 1853-90, in the Stedelijk Museum, Amsterdam, The Netherlands; 'Twelve Sunflowers in a Vase' by Vincent van Gogh, in the Neue Pinakothek, Munich, Germany; 'Self-portrait, 1889' by Vincent van Gogh, in Musée Orsay, Paris, France; 'Seascape at Sainte-

Marie' in the Pushkin Museum, Moscow, USSR; all by courtesy of the Bridgeman Art Library, London, UK. 'Squirrels in a Chennar Tree' (EK 1647) by Abul Hasan; 'Cross Carpet page' (Cotton Nero C.IV f210v) from the Lindisfarne Gospels, by courtesy of the British Library, London, UK. Inuit sculpture of a mother and child; 'The Hunt' by Kitao Masayoshi; 'King Louis Philippe turning into a pear in 4 stages' by Honoré Daumier; 'Hyena mask from the Ibo tribe'; 'Balloon-flower with other plants and cicada' by Kitagawa Utamaro; 'The hollow of the deep sea wave' by Hokusai; 'Frog' by Hoji; 'Elephant' by Rembrandt; 'Artist at Work' by Ando Hiroshige; 'Kyo-Bashi Bridge & Take-Gashi' by Ando Hiroshige; 'False Perspective' by William Hogarth; 'Nebamun's Garden'; 'Child Upsetting a Goldfish Bowl' by Kitagawa Utamaro; 'Crocodile' and 'Gazi Riding on a Tiger'; 'Soldiers Swimming a Moat to Escape from King Ashurnasirpal', an Assyrian frieze; 'The Weighing of the Heart' and 'The Four Baboons' from the Egyptian Book of the Dead of Ani; 'The Lion and Antelope playing Senet'; all by courtesy of the Trustees of the British Museum, London, UK. 'Landscape' by Diaz de la Peña, by courtesy of the Fitzwilliam Museum, Cambridge, UK. Self-portrait by Albrecht Dürer, by courtesy of Graphische Sammlung Albertina, Vienna, Austria. 'The Statue of Liberty' by courtesy of Greg Evans Photo Library, London, UK. 'Recumbent Figure' by Henry Moore, by courtesy of the Henry Moore Foundation, Hertfordshire, UK. 'Malaysian shadow puppets' by courtesy of the Horniman Museum, Forest Hill, London, UK. 'Harold's Oath to William' and 'Harold's Return to England' from the Bayeux Tapestry, from the Collection of the Musée de Bayeux, © Michael Holford Photographs, Essex, UK. 'Sassandra Mask from the Ivory Coast' by courtesy of the Musée de l'Homme, Paris, France. 'White Ram' by courtesy of the Museum of English Naive Art, Bath, UK. 'A Maid combing a woman's hair' by Edgar Degas; 'Jesus opens the eyes of a man born blind' by Duccio di Buoninsegna; 'Tropical Storm with a Tiger' by Henri Rousseau; 'The Arnolfini Marriage' by Jan van Eyck; 'Landscape with Psyche Outside the Palace of Cupid' by Claude Lorraine; 'A Seaport' by Claude Lorraine; 'Rain, Steam and Speed' by JMW Turner; all by courtesy of the Trustees, the National Gallery, London, UK. 'Sir Henry Unton' (artist unknown), by courtesy of the National Portrait Gallery, London, UK. 'A Great White Heron' by John James Audubon, by courtesy of the Natural History Museum, London, UK. 'Moses Marcy in a Landscape', overmantel panel (artist unknown), LB 19942/Henry E Peach, by courtesy of Old Sturbridge Village, Massachusetts, USA. 'January' and 'October' from 'Les Très Riches Heures du Duc de Berry', by Pol de Limbourg, in Musée Condé, by courtesy of Photographie Giraudon, Paris, France. The Great Buddha, photograph by Nigel Blythe, by courtesy of Robert Harding Picture Library, London, UK. 'Sketches of Cats' by Leonardo da Vinci, by courtesy of Windsor Castle, UK, Royal Library, © HM The Queen. 'The Snail' by Henri Matisse; 'Boulogne Sands' by Philip Wilson Steer, by courtesy of the Tate Gallery, London, UK. Terracotta Warriors from Xian, China, by courtesy of Tony Stone Photolibrary, London, UK. 'Woman and chrysanthemums' by Utagawa Kuniyoshi; 'Girl with apple' by Isaac Oliver; William de Morgan tile design; 'Strawberry Thief' by William Morris; 'Turkey Cock' by Mansur; 'Akbar Entering Surat', a Mughal miniature; 'Ships Entering Tempozan Harbour' by Yashima Gakutei; 'Visiting a Friend in the Mountains'; 'Rolling up the Blinds to Look at Plum Blossom' by Kitagawa Utamaro; 'Rejoicing at the Birth of Prince Salim', a Mughal Miniature; Chinese Dragon Robe; Persian Carpet; 'The Foxe and the Raysyns' by Anton Sorg; 'The Cockerel and the Pearl' by Kano Tomonobu; all by courtesy of the Board of Trustees of the Victoria & Albert Museum, London, UK. 'Ruins of Holyrood Chapel' by Louis Daguerre, by courtesy of the Walker Art Gallery, Liverpool, UK. 'The Christening Feast' by Jan Steen by courtesy of the Trustees, the Wallace Collection, London, UK. Aboriginal bark painting; North American totem pole, both by courtesy of the Werner Forman Archive, London, UK.

The publishers would like to give special thanks to staff at the Victoria & Albert Museum, London, and to Floyd Beckford and his colleagues at the British Museum, London.